KB202857

Seon Master Daehaeng

The Diamond Sutra:

The Great
Unfolding

대행큰스님의 뜻으로 푼 금강경

hanmaum

대행큰스님의 뜻으로 푼 금강경

발 행 일 2025년 1월 30일
한글번역 대행큰스님
영문번역 한마음국제문화원
디 자 인 박수연
발   행 한마음출판사
출판등록 384-2000-000010
전화 (031) 470-3175
팩스 (031) 470-3209
이메일 onemind@hanmaum.org
www.hanmaumbooks.org
www.hanmaum.org

ISBN 978-89-91857-90-2(03220)

The Diamond Sutra: The Great Unfolding
Seon Master Daehaeng

Copyright © 2025 Hanmaum Seonwon Foundation

Korean Translation by Seon Master Daehaeng
English Translation by Hanmaum International Culture Institute
Design by Su Yeon Park
Published by Hanmaum Publications
www.hanmaumbooks.org

ISBN 978-89-91857-90-2(03220)
Printed in the Republic of Korea
January 2025 Edition

Contents

목차

여는 글 Introduction   11

금강경 번역 후 삼막사 산책을 다녀오시며
Upon returning from a walk in the
mountains after finishing translating
the *Diamond Sutra* into Korean   23

序: 한마음의 세계에 들어서다
Sharing the Energy of the Whole   29

1. 법을 설한 까닭은   33   The circumstances of this teaching

2. 선현善現이 법을 청하니   37   Subhuti asks to be taught

3. 대승의 바른 종지를   45   Essentials of the all-encompassing Great Vehicle

4. 안과 밖이 둘 아닌 행이 아니라면
묘행과 중용이 아니니라   51   The middle path and marvelous actions both arise from functioning as one mind, with no distinctions of inner or outer

5. 심안으로 옳게 보아야 하느니   61   You have to see correctly through the mind's eye

6. 바른 믿음은 나의 뿌리, 즉 자성부터이니라   65   Your root, your inherent nature, is the source of true faith

7. 얻을 것도 없고 설할 것도 없음이라   75   Nothing to gain, nothing to teach

8. 법에 의해 생산이 되나니   81   Everything arises from the functioning of one mind, this nondual whole

9. 일체 상쒜이 상이 아님이니   87   What you see isn't what you are seeing

10. 둘 아닌 공심, 즉 한자리인 것이니   103   This nondual mind, which is everything working together as one

11. 무위공덕이 제일 높음이오니   111   The virtue and merit that arises through the intangible, boundless functioning of one mind is unsurpassed

12. 바르게 가르침을 존중함이니 **119** Correctly teaching these verses is recognized throughout all realms

13. 법답게 받아 지님이니 **125** Know that these teachings describe the underlying principles of how all things function, and deeply engrave them in your heart

14. 상相을 떠나야 적멸함이니라 **137** Ultimate tranquility comes after leaving behind fixed ideas and views

15. 선과 경을 둘이 아니게 지닌 공덕은 자유로워서 **161** The virtue and merit that comes from embracing the teachings and inner spiritual practice as one is beyond imagining and reaches everywhere

16. 능히 이러하다면 업장 굴레에서 벗어나리라 **177** Anyone who can thoroughly do this will free themselves from the chains of karma

17. 끝 간 데 없이 내가 없음이라 **189** At no point is there "I"

18. 일체 만물만생을 둘 아니게 봄이니 **213** Seeing absolutely everything nondually

19. 법계를 두루 찰나찰나 화함이니라 **225** Becoming one with the entire Dharma realm and ceaselessly manifesting far and wide

20. 색色과 상相을 여윔이니 **231** Breaking away from appearances and perceptions

21. 마음과 마음으로 통하는 설법이니라 **237** Teachings that come from mind, connecting with mind

22. 일체 법이 공하여 고정됨이 없이 화하여 그냥 여여한 까닭에 얻을 것이 없음이니라 **243** All things are connected through the foundation, and function as one whole, ceaselessly transforming, with no fixed form, and are just flowing without hindrance. Thus, there is nothing to gain.

23. 내면과 물질세계가
둘이 아닌 마음으로 선善을 행함이니 247 Realizing that all inner and outer
things work together nondually, go
forward putting this into practice

24. 복덕도 지혜도 둘이 아니었음이니라 253 Both the wisdom and the good
fortune that result from nondual
actions and thought turn out to be
ultimately the same thing

25. 교화하되 교화함이 없이 함이니 259 Teaching and guiding through the
foundation, with no giver or receiver

26. 법신은 상相이 아님이니라 265 The manifestations of Tathagata do
not have fixed forms

27. 끊는 것도 없고 멸함도 없음이니 273 There is no "ceasing" or
"extinguishing"

28. 받지도 않고 탐하지도 않음이니 279 Neither receiving nor coveting

29. 위없는 고요함이니   287   Ultimate serenity

30. 끝없는 진리와 현상은 하나임이니   291   All phenomena are the ceaseless workings of everything as one whole

31. 지견을 내지 않음이니   299   Not giving rise to thoughts of "knowing"

32. 천백억화신이 응신이 되어 만 중생에게 자비 보시를 천차만별로 응하시니 함이 없이 하심이네   305   Unconditionally helping every kind of being by responding from the whole in billions of different ways

315   결結: 꽃이 피고 열매 맺어 Blossoming and Ripening

319   닫는 글   Afterword

325   대행큰스님에 대하여 About Seon Master Daehaeng

여는 글

이 책은 『금강경』의 뜻을 한글로 풀어 놓은 대행큰스님의 자필 원본을 기본으로 하여 영역英譯한 것입니다. 금강경이라는 경전의 명칭은 구마라집 스님의 한역漢譯본(CE.401)에서 유래한 것으로 산스크리트 원전의 제목은 "금강능단반야바라밀경金剛能斷般若波羅密經"으로 옮길 수 있습니다.

'금강'은 우리의 근본마음, 불성, 본래 성품을 비유하며, 금강석과 같이 한없이 밝고 단단하여 그 어떤 것으로도 부서지지 않고 파괴되지 않는 특성을 지칭합니다. '능단'이란 번뇌와 집착, 무명과 업식을 천둥번개처럼 능히 순식간에 끊어버릴 수 있음을 의미하지요. '반야'란 판단능력이나 분별력 같은 통상적인 의미의 지혜가 아니라 깊은 수행의 과정을 통해 세상의 이치를 있는 그대로 아는 것, 최상승의 지혜인 깨달음을 가리키며, '바라밀'은 열반의 세계, 즉 마음의 궁극의 상태에 도달하게 됨을 일컫는 말입니다.

Introduction

This English translation is based on the handwritten version of Seon Master Daehaeng's vernacular Korean translation of Kumarajiva's edition of the *Diamond Sutra*. Its original Sanskrit title is the *Vajracchedika prajnaparamita sutra*.

Even the title exudes wisdom: *Vajra*, which is translated as "Diamond," symbolizes our fundamental mind, our original Buddha nature. It highlights the inherent characteristics of this nature, describing it as infinitely bright, indestructible, and capable of cutting through anything.

Chedika means taking any kind of clinging, ignorance, or karmic states of consciousnesses, and throwing it off in an instant, like the crash of a lightning bolt.

Prajna refers to ultimate wisdom. This isn't the ability to judge or discern that we use in daily life, but rather the fundamental wisdom, the infinitely bright supreme wisdom of emptiness, which allows us to understand all the functioning of the world, and which can only be obtained through deep spiritual practice.

요약하자면, 『금강경』은 우리가 수행을 통해 무지와 어리석음을 걷어냈을 때 이르게 되는 대자유의 깨달음의 세계를 보여주는 불교 최고의 경전입니다.

그렇기에, 금강경은 반야심경과 함께 가장 많이 읽히고 가장 많이 독송되고 있는 경전임에도 거기에 담긴 뜻이 매우 심오하고 정교하여 관습적인 사고로는 이해하기 어렵습니다. 통상적인 차원을 넘어선 논리와 뜻으로 가득 채워져 있기 때문이지요. 금강경의 이러한 특성으로 인해 다양한 해석을 담고 있는 번역서와 주석서가 다수 존재하게 되었습니다.

대행큰스님은 불이법의 지혜를 이미 깨달은 선지식의 시각으로 경전에 다가갔고, 짧지만 명료한 시적인 해석으로 분별없이 하나로 같이 돌아가는 광대한 마음의 이치를 느끼게 해줌으로써 금강경의 본질이 무엇인지 보여주고 있습니다. 큰스님의 뜻으로 푼 『금강경』에는 셀 수도 없이 많은 지혜와 깊은 뜻이 곳곳에 담겨 있지만, 다음과 같은 두가지 측면은 특히 더 두드러진다고 하겠습니다.

보이는 세계와 보이지 않는 세계가 둘 아니게 같이 돌아가고

대행큰스님은 이 세계가 돌아가는 이치가 마음에 방점을 찍고 있음을 금강경 서두부터 확실하게 보여줍니다. 금강경 제1분 첫 소절을 큰스님은 "만법이

Paramita represents the state of completeness, which opens the door to nirvana.

In short, the *Diamond Sutra* is an embodiment of bright, nondual wisdom that shows us the world of great freedom and sublime awareness, which we can realize when we strive through spiritual practice to transcend ignorance and its related behaviors.

This depth has led the *Diamond Sutra* to become one of the most widely read and recited sutras of Mahayana Buddhism. However, because its meaning is so subtle and profound, describing the awareness and functioning of dimensions beyond ordinary, dualistic perceptions, its logic does not yield to conventional thinking. This aspect of the sutra has led to a great many commentaries and translations over the centuries.

Seon Master Daehaeng approaches the sutra from the perspective of one who has already awakened to this nondual wisdom, and thus is able to leave the reader with a sense of the functioning of this great, inherent wholeness. In such a rich and profound atmosphere, there are innumerable nuggets of wisdom and streams of meaning, but two, in particular, stand out.

The visible and the unseen working together as one

Throughout the *Diamond Sutra*, Seon Master Daehaeng focuses on the intertwined functioning of the seen and unseen, of what in Korean is sometimes called "one mind." Because people are already well aware of the material and visible aspects of existence, she

둘 아닌 한마음을 통해 들고 남을 나는 들었노라. 부처님께서는 일심이 만법,
만법이 일심이라 하셨다"고 번역했습니다. 지금까지, 경전의 첫 문장의 뜻을
이렇게 명확하게 살려낸 금강경 해석서는 없었습니다.

이것은 일종의 선언입니다. 이 세상은 마음이 있기에 존재하는 것이며, 우리
는 물질계의 현상속에서만 살아가는 게 아니라는 것을 깨우쳐 알려주는 강력
한 메시지로 시작하는 것이지요. 다시 말해, 물질계와 정신계가 둘 아니게 같
이 돌아가고 있는 실재實在가 사실은 우리들 삶의 바탕이며, 보이지는 않으나
엄연히 존재하여 작동하고 있는 마음의 세계, 즉 정신계의 원리를 제대로 알
아야만이 우리가 진정한 의미에서의 참사람, 끝없는 자유인이 될 수 있음을
확언한 것입니다.

한마음으로 같이 돌아가는 이치는 광대하게 펼쳐지니

금강경에서 석가모니 부처님은 수보리에게 많은 이야기를 해주는 것처럼 보
이지만 큰스님은 그것이 다름 아니라 바로 '한마음의 도리'를 일관성 있게 알
려주는 것임을 분명히 하고 있습니다. 우주의 모든 것은 본래부터 공심共心 공
체共體로서 공용共用 공식共食하며 공생共生하는 것이니, 그것은 만물만생 모두
가 근본마음을 가지고 있으며 그 마음을 통해 서로 연결돼 분별없이 둘 아니
게 돌아가기 때문입니다.

makes a particular emphasis on the role of the unseen and invisible functioning of this one mind.

She makes it abundantly clear that this is the starting point of all things when she translates the first verse of the sutra as, "All things in the universe arise from and return to, function and manifest through this nondual one mind. Thus I have perceived." In the very next paragraph, she continues, saying that Buddha "…taught that one mind is the source of everything, and that all things and energies function as one through one mind."

With this statement, Seon Master Daehaeng is telling us quite explicitly that the visible world is not the totality of existence, nor are we beings who live in a world made up of only the material and phenomenal. Instead, she tells us, we are the interconnected functioning of our deep connection with the whole. And while this connection and its functioning remain unseen, we must become aware of this and learn how it works. For only in this way can we live as a whole person and a free person, regardless of the circumstances that may arise.

The great unfolding of the whole

In Seon Master Daehaeng's *Diamond Sutra*, she makes it clear that the focus of Shakyamuni Buddha's teachings is the principle of one mind. Through this energy, this one mind, we are directly connected with each and every other life and form, and are ceaselessly functioning together. And in the midst of this vast energy of one

이렇게 광대하게 돌아가는 이 어마어마한 무상無常의 장場에서는 그 어떤 것도 머물러 있지 않습니다. 당연히 '나'라든지 '내가 했다'라는 것이 있을 수 없습니다. 규정된 시간도 공간도 없기에 규정된 차원도 없습니다. 이 세상에 모든 것은 인연 화합으로 생겨났다 사라지며, 변하지 않는 것은 아무 것도 없습니다. 그저 끊임없이 변화하며 둘 아니게 같이 돌아갈 뿐이지요. 그렇기에 그 어떤 것에도 집착할 게 없다는 것입니다.

이러한 상태를 큰스님은 공空이라 표현하였습니다. 아무 것도 없어 텅 비었다는 뜻이 아니라, 찰나찰나 변해 돌아가며 셀 수도 없이 많은 것이 꽉 차 있음을 뜻하여 공이라 한 것입니다. 금강경 설법의 핵심인 공한 한마음의 이치를 큰스님은 경전 전체를 마무리하는 결結 부분에서 "갖은 꽃이 갖은 꽃이 피고 지고 피고 지고…"로 시작하는 한 편의 선시禪詩로 아름답게 묘사합니다. 이 시의 구절들은 깨달음을 얻은 선지식의 지혜가 아니었더라면 도저히 표현해 낼 수 없는 우아함을 드러내 보여주고, 이 세상 전체가 함께 돌아가는 참된 진리를 매우 간결하면서도 웅장하게 종결지어 주면서, 경전 해석의 진수를 보여줍니다.

대자유인이 되어 진정한 평안으로

대행큰스님의 뜻으로 푼 『금강경』은 흔들리지 않고 불안해하지 않아도 되는

mind, there is no "I" that exists apart. There is no separate chunk that can be set aside, because inherently all beings are connected as one – communicating, living, working together, and nourishing each other as one.

In the ceaseless flowing and changing that is this impermanence of one mind, there isn't the least trace of "I did," because everything involved has already changed and flowed away. Everything in this world arises and disappears within a web of cause and effect, with no instant that it is not ceaselessly changing. In the midst of this flowing, there is no moment or form that remains unchanged. There is no independently existing "I," and no separately existing time or space, and so there are also no independently existing dimensions. What would you cling to, and what need is there to cling to anything?

Seon Master Daehaeng describes this ever-flowing nature of all things as "Emptiness." It is not an emptiness where there is nothing, but rather a ceaselessly changing, ever-flowing whole that has no separate pieces that could be grasped and held up as a "thing." It is "empty" of all labels and dualistic divisions. After the last chapter of the *Diamond Sutra*, she adds a verse that beautifully describes this emptiness of one mind, saying, "Flowers of every kind bloom and fade, bloom and fade, fade and bloom, at last bearing fruit." This verse elegantly and concisely describes the truth of this world of the mind and the richness of this flowing whole.

당당한 삶을 영위할 수 있는 길로 우리를 안내합니다. 또한 남을 살리는 일이 바로 나를 살리는 일이 되는 진정한 사랑이 무엇인지 가르쳐 줍니다.

이 세상 모든 것에는 근본마음이 있습니다. 눈에는 보이지 않고 손으로 잡을 수는 없지만, 우리는 이 근본마음을 통해 연결돼 있어서 나와 상대가 둘 아니게 만물만생과 서로 소통하고 도우며 참다운 인간으로서의 삶을 살아 갈 수 있습니다. 그러니 나의 근본마음을 믿고 근심, 걱정, 기쁨, 슬픔, 행복 전부를 거기에 내려놓고 가보세요. 보이지 않는 자리가 오히려 나를 받쳐주고 지탱해 주고 살려내는 것을 체험하게 될 겁니다. 더 나아가 이 책에서 알려주는 궁극의 도리를 몸소 깨닫는다면 대자유인이 되어 진정한 평안에 다다르게 될 것입니다. 이전에는 전혀 상상해보지 못했을 금강경의 세계를 체험해 볼 수 있는 뜻 깊은 여정에 여러분 모두를 초대합니다.

한마음국제문화원 일동 합장

Discovering ourselves through our connection with others

Seon Master Daehaeng's awakened translation of the *Diamond Sutra* shows us the path to becoming a true human being, where we can experience a dignified life free of anxiety, as well as a compassionate life in which saving others becomes saving myself.

She explains that there is a foundation to all the world, and although it is invisible to the eye and cannot be grasped by the hand, through it we are connected to all other lives and things. As we begin to rely upon this connection, entrusting it with our worries and hardships, the problems we face and our hopes for the future, along with all of our thoughts of "I" and "you," this foundation responds to us. As we go forward testing this and experimenting with it, we can overcome seemingly impossible obstacles, learn how to truly help others, and discover what love fully means.

We invite you to experience this world of the *Diamond Sutra* and step forward into a journey you never imagined!

With palms together,
The Hanmaum International Culture Institute

그러습니다 세존이시여 ㊶ 바라옵건대 즐거이 듣고자 하옵니다

㊷ 대승이 바른 종지를 ㊸ 부처님께서 수보리에게 말씀하셨다

㊹ 내변이모든 자생중생이 내마음과 돌아느줄알면 항복바든 것이니라

㊺ 만물만생의 진차 만별이 종기인걸

㊻ 난생태생 습생 화생이 돌아는걸 유약무색 유상무상이 교 정됨이없나

잘아 잘아 화하여 돌아나게 황하여시방이 초월하얀느다

나없는나는 다 무심에 들게하며 ㊾ 열반별도서 ㊿ 내가있고 내가 하는게야

㊼ 일천 만물 만생이 별도가 된다해도 52 무순가닭인가 수보리야 54)끝보...

49 별도를 얻을수는 없쓰리라 53 아상 인상 중생상 수좌상이 있으면 54

51 떡도를

53 만약)보살일이

A handwritten page from Seon Master Daehaeng's original manuscript.

일러두기
이 책의 금강경 한글본은 2023년 발행된 『대행스님의 뜻으로 푼 금강경』을 참고하였으며,
대행큰스님의 금강경 뜻풀이 자필 원문을 근간으로 삼았습니다. 따라서 2023년 발행된
『대행스님의 뜻으로 푼 금강경』과는 다소 차이가 있을 수 있습니다.

Seon Master Daehaeng

The Diamond Sutra:
The Great Unfolding

대행큰스님의 뜻으로 푼 금강경

금강경 번역 후
삼막사 산책을
다녀오시며…

대행큰스님
1993. 8. 7.

천지인天地人

우주의 천차만별이

한 찰나에 벌어졌다

한 찰나에 모였다 흩어지는

이 광대한 산하대지에

산천초목은

장단 맞추어 음파를 두루두루 전달하고

나의 노래 소리와 더불어

전 우주 봉우리마다

허탈하게 웃으며

Upon returning from a walk in the mountains
after finishing translating
the Diamond Sutra *into Korean*

Seon Master Daehaeng
August 7, 1993

The heavens and the Earth and human beings,

every kind of thing in the universe

is unfolding every instant,

constantly gathering together and separating.

All across this vast land,

the mountains and rivers,

the flowers and trees,

all follow this rhythm,

spreading this cadence far and wide.

Singing along with this,

a quiet laugh

arises from within me

and from within every great peak[1] of the universe.

1
Great peak: Every great peak of the universe implies awakened beings throughout all realms, so the nuance is that the same thing was said by all great beings, arising from a place of oneness where past, present, and future are all one.

이래도 한세상

저래도 한세상

일체 색과 모든 생이

한꺼번에 끝없이 이어지며

나의 한마음의 웃음소리는

삼천대천세계 우주를 흔들며

물방울마다 향기 내음 되고

꽃송이마다 열매 되어

무루無漏 유루有漏 제대로 익어서

일체 생들이

그릇대로 끝없는 삶을 노래하네.

Take this path,

and everything is working together as one,

take that path,

and everything still works together as one.

Every life and thing in this world,

just keeps unfolding together,

on and on, endlessly.

The laughter of my one mind [2]

reverberates throughout

all realms of the universe,

causing every drop of water

to give off a sweet fragrance,

and every blossom to transform into fruit,

ripening everything

throughout all the unseen dimensions,

as well as all the visible realms,

so that every being sings

this song of endless unfolding,

each according to its role.

[2]
One mind: (Hanmaum [han-ma-um]) From the Korean, where "one" has a nuance of great and combined, and "mind" is more than intellect, and includes "heart" as well. Together, they mean everything combined and connected as one.

What is called "one mind" is intangible, unseen, and has no divisions of time or space. It has no beginning or end, and is sometimes called our fundamental mind. It also means the flowing whole, where all beings and everything in the universe are connected together and functioning as one.

이러해도 한세상

저러해도 한세상인데

나로부터

상대의 우주 섭류의 정신계에

광대한 마음과 마음이 이어지는 도리를

한데 합쳐 깨달으면

끝없는 자유인이 되리라.

If you take this path,

everything works together as one.

If you take that path,

everything works together as one,

but if you can awaken to this great unfolding whole for yourself,

where everything in the universe

is functioning as one, through one mind,

each connected to the other,

realizing that all of this is happening here,

together with your foundation, your fundamental mind,

then forevermore,

you will be free,

free,

truly free.

한마음의 세계에 들어서다

대행큰스님

자아궁위^{自我宮衛}의 일체를 지혜로

도리천원에 드시어

큰, 한마음의 불바퀴와

천지인^{天地人}과 함께 하셨다.

그때 세존께서 일체 생과 함께

재식^{齋食} 법의 공양하실 때라

옷 아닌 옷을 입고

활궁발우^{活宮鉢盂}를 드시고

들고 남이 없이

자아궁으로 드시어

재식하시려고

28

Sharing the Energy of the Whole

Seon Master Daehaeng

Through the vast, bright wisdom of inherent nature,

the Buddha[3] Shakyamuni entered the great flowing

and connecting energy of one mind,

where he became one with

the heavens and the earth and human beings.

Having taken form in the human realm,

when it was time for the midday meal,

that is to say,

when it was time to gather and share energy

with all beings,

the World-honored One

put on clothes that were not clothes,

and took up his bowl,

the bowl of mind,

where a single thought entrusted to this foundation

transforms and manifests into the world,

becoming reality.

[3]
Buddha: The word
used in Korean is also
describing someone who
has become one with all
the lives of their body,
and transformed them
into bodhisattvas.

자아궁천에서 차근차근

재식 공양을 얻은 사이 없이 얻으시어

두 자리 아닌 자리로 돌아오시어

재식 공양을 한마음으로 마치시고

의발衣鉢아닌 의발을 거두시고

일체 발이 둘 아닌 뒤에

평등공법平等空法 자리에 앉으셨다.

Holding this bowl,

he entered the bright energy of true, inherent nature,

without any aspect of coming or going.

With the intent of sharing the energy of the whole

with all beings,

he calmly gathered this bright energy of inherent nature,

gathering it with no moment of "gathering."

He returned to the place that is not two places,

and there,

one with everything, shared the energy of the whole.

Having finished,

he took off the robe that was not a robe,

put away the bowl that was not a bowl,

and, making the feet of all beings his own feet,

he seated himself in the great emptiness,

the interconnected flowing that

encompasses everything

and is the underlying functioning of all the universe.

01 / 법을 설한 까닭은

chapter 1

The circumstances of this teaching

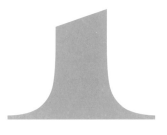

1. 법을 설한 까닭은

만법이 둘 아닌 한마음을 통해 들고 남을

나는 들었노라.

한때 부처님께서 사위국을 세우시고

일심이 만법, 만법이 일심이라 하시니

큰 비구들 천이백오십 인과 함께하셨다.

그때 세존께서 공양하실 때라

옷을 입고 발우를 드시고

사위성으로 들어가시어 걸식하시는데

그 성안에서 차례로 밥을 얻어서

다시 본래 자리로 돌아오시어

공양을 마치시고 의발을 거두시고

발을 씻으신 뒤에 자리를 펴고 앉으셨다.

All things in the universe arise from and return to,
function and manifest through this nondual one mind.
Thus I have perceived.

As the Buddha was building Shravasti,[4]

he taught that one mind

is the source of everything,

and that all things and energies

function as one through one mind.[5]

Gathered there together with him were

1,250 great bhikkhus.

When it was time for meals,

the Buddha would put on robes,

take up his bowl,

and go into the city with the other bhikkhus,

going from house to house,

collecting food offerings.

Returning, he would eat his meal,

put away his robe and bowl,

wash his feet,

and arrange himself on his seat.

4

Building Shravasti: The Korean is very deliberate in this expression. Shravasti was already a major city at this time, so the implication here is that it was the spiritual foundations of the city that the Buddha was building.

5

...through one mind: One of the implications of this sentence is that a single thought raised from our one mind will spread out and manifest into the world. Likewise, all aspects of everything we encounter, both pleasant and unpleasant, will, when entrusted to this one mind, be embraced and changed by this energy, and go forward in a way that furthers growth.

02 / 선현善現이 법을 청하니

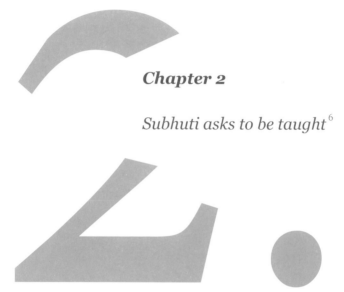

Chapter 2

Subhuti asks to be taught [6]

---

[6] **Subhuti's request**: In the *Diamond Sutra*, Subhuti is speaking from a desire to understand how an awakened practitioner can help other beings move forward. So in this chapter, he wants to confirm his understanding of how he can truly help others, both directly and by helping unawakened beings to understand this teaching for themselves.

2. 선현善現이 법을 청하니

그때 장로 수보리가

대중 가운데 있다가 자리에서 일어나

오른쪽 어깨에 옷을 걷어 메고

오른쪽 무릎을 땅에 꿇어 합장 공경하며

부처님께 사뢰었다.

희유하십니다, 세존이시여.

여래께서는 한마음의 자생화신보살들을

둘 아니게 다스리시며

한마음의 자생응신보살들의 둘 아닌 굴림이십니다.

O ne day,
after their meal,
the preeminent bhikkhu, Subhuti,
arose from his place among those gathered near the Buddha.
He covered his right shoulder with his robe,
placed his right knee on the ground,
and kneeling thus, with his palms together,
spoke:

"How rare, oh World-honored One!

Tathagata[7] nondually guides and

directs the manifestation

of one mind as innumerable bodhisattvas.

Their response and interaction with

the world are likewise

the nondual functioning of Tathagata.

[7]
Tathagata: While
"Tathagata" is often taken
as another name for the
Buddha, its fundamental
meaning is "the combined
oneness of everything."
So, in many instances,
teachings or statements
aren't spoken by the
Buddha as an individual,
but are arising out from
this combined oneness.

세존이시여,

지혜로운 남녀가 위없는 진실을 깨침에

오방五方의 무상을

걸림 없이 대처하는 마음이시며

내면 자생과 둘 아닐 때 항복이라 하시며,

나 아님 없을 때

마음 없는 마음이

찰나찰나 응신으로 나투리라 하셨나이다.

"World-honored One,

if I have understood correctly,

you have taught us that

when men and women awaken to the deepest truth,

they are able to respond

positively, wisely, proactively,

to the impermanence of every place and thing,

of every life and creation.

As they become one with the unenlightened beings

within their body,

all of those beings naturally submit to and follow one mind.

And with everything perceived as 'myself,'

this nondual mind manifests every moment,

sending forth whatever is needed."

부처님께서 말씀하셨다.

착하도다 착하도다, 수보리야.

네 말과 같이

여래는 안과 밖이 둘 아닌 마음이라

내면 자생보살들은 화신·응신의 나툼을 잘 다스리느니라.

너는 지금 자세히 들어라.

마땅히 너를 위해 말하리라.

지혜로운 남녀가

위없는 진실을 깨우쳐 마음을 낸다면

내면의 자생중생들을 둘 아니게 다스려야 하느니라.

내면의 한마음 없는 한마음을 항복받게 하라.

그렇습니다, 세존이시여.

바라옵건대 즐거이 듣고자 하옵니다.

"Such compassion, Subhuti! Such compassion!"

replied the Buddha.

"It is as you have said.

Tathagata is itself nondual mind,

without discriminations or divisions,

thus innumerable bodhisattvas arise from this one mind,

freely manifesting and responding to whatever is needed.

"Now, listen carefully, and I'll tell you something special:

Those wonderful men and women

who wish to awaken to the deepest truth and

use that to help other beings,

must manage the lives within nondually.

You must take these inner lives that are unaware of one mind,

and cause them to surrender to one mind."

"Thank you, World-honored One!

Your words fill me with joy!

Would you please speak more about this?"

03 / 대승의 바른 종지를

Chapter 3

Essentials of the all-encompassing Great Vehicle[8]

[8] **Great Vehicle:** : This is the "Great Vehicle," or Mahayana, where everything forms one interconnected, flowing whole.

부처님께서 수보리에게 말씀하셨다.

내면의 모든 자생중생이

내 마음과 둘 아닌 줄 알면

항복 받은 것이니라.

만물만생 천차만별의 종류인 것

난생 · 태생 · 습생 · 화생이 둘 아닌 것

유색 · 무색 · 유상 · 무상이

고정됨이 없이

찰나찰나 화하여

둘 아니게 공하여

시공이 초월하였느니라.

The Buddha spoke thus to Subhuti:

"The moment you truly realize that

all of the inner lives within you

are not separate from your fundamental mind,

all of those lives immediately submit to

and follow your fundamental mind.

"All of these beings,

whether born from eggs or wombs,

moisture or transformation,

are all inherently connected as one.

All of these beings,

whether material or immaterial,

whether having form or being formless,

are all ceaselessly changing and transforming,

functioning as one flowing whole,

with no divisions of time or place.

나 없는 나는

다 무심에 들게 하여 열반멸도涅槃滅度에 들게 하리라.

일체 만물만생이 멸도가 된다 해도

내가 있고

내가 하는 게 있다면

멸도를 얻을 수는 없으리라.

무슨 까닭인가, 수보리야.

만약 보살이

아상我相 · 인상人相 · 중생상衆生相 · 수자상壽者相이 있으면

곧 보살이 아니니라.

"Thus, this fundamental self that isn't 'me'

can guide all of these lives to the state

where there is no separate 'I,'

where there is only flowing,

and from there

to enter nirvana.[9]

However, even though all other beings have reached nirvana,

if you still have thoughts of 'I,'

'I am,' 'I am doing,'

then nirvana will be unattainable.

"Why is this, Subhuti?

Should even a bodhisattva

give rise to ideas of themselves as existing apart from others,

or feel that they have achieved a level of spiritual evolution,

or think that some beings exist at lower states of development,

or that their spiritual work is constrained by time or space,

then, as soon as they think such things,

they cannot fulfill the role of a bodhisattva."

04 /

안과 밖이 둘 아닌 행이 아니라면
묘행과 중용이 아니니라

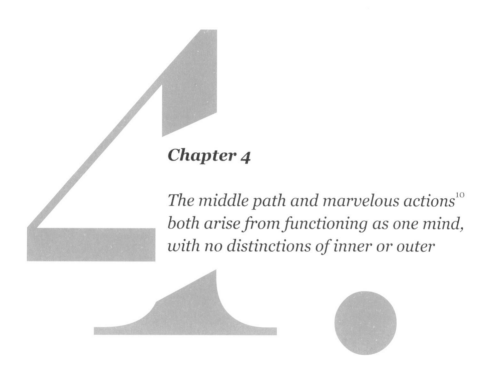

Chapter 4

*The middle path and marvelous actions[10]
both arise from functioning as one mind,
with no distinctions of inner or outer*

[10] **Middle Path**: This describes the state of being where one is able to go forward free of discriminations.
Marvelous Actions: This describes the profound and so-called "miraculous" functioning of the energy of our one mind as it functions together with both the visible and the unseen realms.

그리고 수보리야,

보살은 법에 의해 마땅히 함이 없이

조건 없이 자비행을 할지니라.

이른바 모습을 보지 말고

진실한 마음으로 보시하라.

감촉이나 남의 말에도 속지 말고,

진실한 마음만이 조건 없이 보시할 수 있느니라.

" **F**urther, Subhuti,
bodhisattvas,

now able to function as one with everything,

and perceiving their connection with uncountable beings

and the unimaginable support and aid they've received over eons,

should offer loving help unconditionally,

free of thoughts of 'I' or 'I did.'

To put this another way,

help others without being caught up in their appearances,

and offer aid wholeheartedly.

Don't be caught up in your senses

nor deceived by other's words,

for only your utterly sincere, all-embracing mind

is capable of helping people unconditionally.

수보리야,

보살은 정신계와 물질계가 둘이 아닌 까닭에

그대로 보시이니라.

내가 있느니 내가 했느니 하면

자유인이 아니다.

무슨 까닭인가?

만약 내가 없이 보시한다면

그 공덕은 헤아릴 수 없음이니라.

"Subhuti,

the material realm and spiritual realm

are not two.

Bodhisattvas have realized this

and function accordingly,

so everything they do,

all their actions

benefit, sustain, and support

all the world.

If they had any thought of 'I am,' or 'I did,'

then they could not function thus,

as a truly free being.[11]

Why?

Because it is working without

any trace of 'I'

that gives rise to the unimaginable

virtue and merit[12] that is capable

of benefiting others in any circumstances.

11
Free being:
In this context, a truly free person is someone who is one with their foundation, not controlled by circumstances or karmic states of consciousness, and able to work together as one with every being they meet.

12
Virtue and merit(功德):
Here this term refers to the results of helping unconditionally and non-dually, without any thought of self or other. It becomes virtue and merit when it is "done without doing," that is, done without the thought that "I did." Because it is done unconditionally, all beings benefit from it.

수보리야, 어떻게 생각하느냐

동쪽 허공을 가히 생각으로 헤아릴 수 있겠느냐?

없겠나이다, 세존이시여.

수보리야,

남서북방 사방상하 허공을 생각으로 헤아릴 수 있겠느냐?

없겠나이다, 세존이시여.

"Subhuti,

if you look to the sky in the East,

are your thoughts capable of grasping

everything that's happening there,

throughout all the seen and unseen realms?"

"No, World-honored One, such a thing is not possible."

"If you look to the North, South, or West,

if you look at the heavens,

if you look at the earth,

can your thoughts grasp the arising and disappearing,

the functioning and interactions of this whole?"

"No, World-honored One, they cannot."

수보리야,

나다, 내가 했다 하는 상을 벗어나서 보시하면

공덕이 허공같아

생각으로는 헤아릴 수 없느니라.

수보리야,

뜻과 가르친 대로

내면과 외부가 둘 아닌 마음이라야 하느니라.

"Likewise, Subhuti,

if you help others while free from concepts of 'me' and 'I did,'

your thoughts cannot begin to approach

the vastness of the resulting virtue and merit.

"Subhuti,

as I've just taught you,

as you've already sensed,

and as it has always been,

the key is your one mind.

It is this mind that transcends 'inner' and 'outer,'

embracing everything as one,

which makes possible this middle path

and these marvelous actions."

05 / 심안으로 옳게 보아야 하느니

Chapter 5

You have to see correctly through the mind's eye

수보리야, 어찌 생각하느냐

몸을 보고 여래를 볼 수 있겠느냐?

아니옵니다, 세존이시여.

몸을 보고 여래를 볼 수 없습니다.

무슨 까닭인가 하면

여래께서 말씀하신 바

몸은 곧 몸이 아니니라 하셨습니다.

부처님께서 수보리에게 말씀하셨다.

내면세계와 물질세계를 둘이 아닌 줄 알면

곧 여래를 보리라.

"Subhuti,
what do you think?

When you look at this body, are you seeing Tathagata?"

"No, World-honored One,

Tathagata cannot be seen by looking at you.

Why? Because you have told us that

you, Shakyamuni, are not Tathagata itself,

but rather just a manifestation of Tathagata."

The Buddha then told Subhuti,

"When you truly come to understand

that all the seen and unseen realms,

and their functioning,

are not separate,

then you'll be able to see Tathagata for yourself."

06 /

바른 믿음은 나의 뿌리, 즉 자성부터이니라

Chapter 6

Your root, your inherent nature,
is the source of true faith

수보리가 부처님께 사뢰었다.

세존이시여, 어떤 중생이 이 같은 말씀이나 글귀를 듣고서

진실한 믿음을 내오리까?

부처님께서 수보리에게 말씀하셨다.

그런 말 하지 말라.

여래가 멸도한 후 끝없는 미래에도

각자 마음의 공덕을 닦을 자 있어서

이 글귀에 능히 믿는 마음을 낸다면

나의 마음의 뿌리를 발견하리라.

Subhuti asked the Buddha,

"World-honored One,

will ordinary people

be capable of understanding what you've been saying

and then truly having faith in it?"

The Buddha replied,

"Do not say such things.

Even in the unimaginably distant future,

there will be beings,

who cultivate the virtues grounded in this nondual truth.

If such beings work sincerely and wholeheartedly

at applying these teachings,

they will discover their root,

their fundamental mind.

마땅히 알라.

모든 사람 마음속에

영원한 근본 선근이 본래 심어졌을 뿐 아니라

이미 일체 부처님께

만물만생에게

뿌리, 즉 선근이 심어졌으므로

이 말씀과 글귀를 듣고 나아가

한생각에 진실한 믿음의 마음을 내느니라.

수보리야,

여래는 다 알고 다 보느니라.

일체 중생들이

나로 하여 세상이 있는 것을 안다면

무량 공덕을 얻느니라.

"Pay attention!

Inherently, every person has within them this eternal,

fundamental root.

So, too, does every life, every thing, and every buddha.

All have this wonderful root,

thus, there will be beings who,

after hearing these teachings,

will go forward becoming one with everything they encounter,

responding to it all through their own root.

"Subhuti,

Tathagata is the state where everything

functions as one,

and so perceives and understands all things.

Thus, I can tell you that

if people should realize that,

'My presence creates the world that is unfolding in front of me,'

they will attain

truly endless

virtue and merit.

무슨 까닭인가?

이 모든 중생은

내가 했다, 내가 주었다, 내가 높다 하는 마음이 없다면

법이라는 것도 없고 법이 아니라는 것도 없느니라.

무슨 까닭인가?

모든 중생이

만약 나라는 마음을 세우면

곧 물질세계에 집착함이 되나니,

법을 구한다 해도

곧 아상 · 인상 · 중생상 · 수자상에 집착함이며

법 아님을 취해도 곧 네 가지 상에 집착함이니라.

"Why is this?

When people have no thoughts of 'I did,'

'I gave,' 'I'm better than,'

then they will likewise not be caught by ideas such as

'This is the path' or 'That isn't the path,'

'This is the truth' or 'That isn't the truth.'

"If any beings give rise to ideas of 'I,'

those will lead to attachments to

the world of discriminations.[13]

Even if someone is searching for the truth,

if they give rise to thoughts of 'I'm doing,'

'I am,' and so on,

then those thoughts will cause them

to fall into attachments, to ideas of a separate self,

of having achieved a certain level of evolution,

of others existing at lower states of development,

or of thinking that they are constrained by time or space.

Of course, pursuing things other than the truth

will likewise cause someone to fall into these mistaken views.

13
World of discriminations: The literal word used here is "material realms," but from the context, it appears the focus is on the aspect of the material realms that encourages contrasts, comparisons, and evaluations based on the physical senses.

무슨 까닭인가?

마땅히 법도 법 아님도 취하지 말아야 하며

내면의 양면을 놓으면

불이 켜질 뿐이니라.

이런 뜻인 까닭에 여래가 항상 말하시기를

　　"비구들이여,

　　나의 설법에 내가 없는데 법이 있으랴.

　　법이 없는데 법 아님이 있으랴."

"So, don't get caught up

in what is 'truth' or what is 'not the truth,'

in what is 'the path' or what is 'not the path,'

in what are 'the noble teachings'

or what are 'not the noble teachings.'

Just let go of both sides,

including even your deep understanding of them,

and then the light will come on.

How could it not?

"Thus, Tathagata is always saying,

> *Bhikkhus,*
>
> *in all that I have taught, there is no 'me,'*
>
> *so how there be some other, separate thing called 'truth'?*
>
> *If there is not even 'truth,'*
>
> *how could there be something that is 'not the truth'?"*

07 / 얻을 것도 없고 설할 것도 없음이라

Chapter 7

Nothing to gain, nothing to teach

수보리야,

어떻게 생각하느냐

여래가 위없는 진실한 깨달음을 얻었다고 생각하느냐

여래가 설한 법이 있다고 생각하느냐?

수보리가 말씀드리되

부처님께서 설하신 뜻을 알기에는

눈 귀가 어두워서 볼 수는 없사오나

위없는 진실을 깨달았다 함은

이름일 뿐 법이 아니며

또한 여래가 설하셨다 할 고정된 법도 없습니다.

"Subhuti,
did Tathagata awaken to the greatest, most supreme truth?
And has Tathagata been teaching about this truth?"

Subhuti replied,

"Although my eyes and ears are still dark,

and I haven't clearly seen this for myself,

it appears to me that,

according to what you have explained,

concepts such as

'Awakening to the greatest, most supreme truth'

are just labels,

not the essence itself.

Further, it is impossible to hold something up and say,

'This is what Tathagata has taught.'

무슨 까닭인가 하면,

여래께서 설하신 법은

어떤 것을 했다 안 했다 할 수 없어서

다 취할 바 없으며

말도 할 수 없으며

법도 아니고 법 아님도 아니기 때문입니다.

무슨 까닭인가 하면,

일체 물질세계가

무위법에서 천차만별로 화하여

고정됨이 없기 때문입니다.

"Why?

It can't be said that Tathagata teaches something

or doesn't teach something.

There was never anything to grasp onto,

nothing for opinions to form around,

and nothing that is truth or not the truth.

"Why is this?

It is because all the things of this world

are ceaselessly changing.

They all arise from the endlessly transforming and manifesting,

unseen functioning of the whole."

08 / 법에 의해 생산이 되나니

Chapter 8

Everything arises from the functioning of one mind,
this nondual whole

수보리야, 어떻게 생각하느냐

어떤 사람이

삼천대천세계에 가득한 칠보를

한마음 내어 보시한다면

이 사람이 보시한 대가의 복덕이 얼마나 많겠느냐?

수보리가 말씀드리되

매우 많습니다, 세존이시여.

왜냐하면 공덕이 공덕이 아닌 까닭에

여래께서 공덕이 많다고 말씀하셨습니다.

만약 또 어떤 사람이

이 경 가운데서

사구게를 공한 도리로 받아 지녀서

"Subhuti,
what do you think?

If someone,

while entrusting everything to this one mind and relying upon it,

used all the treasures of the universe to help others,

that would give rise to much good merit, wouldn't it?"

Subhuti answered,

"The merit would be truly vast,

World-honored One.

It would be virtue and merit that transcends virtue and merit,

because it would not be caught in the realm of fixed ideas.

Thus, Tathagata describes it as 'much.'"

"Likewise, Subhuti,

should someone,

understanding that these verses are describing

the interconnected, flowing whole,

work at reflecting upon them and applying them,

만물만생을 둘 아니게 설한다면

공덕 아닌 공덕이 될 것이니라.

수보리야,

왜냐하면 일체제불의 한마음은,

위없이 진실한 밝음의 한마음의 법이

모든 경으로부터

한마음과 둘 아니게 발전을 이루나니

수보리야,

말하자면 불법이,

불법 아닌 불법이

그대로 일체 생활이니라.

teaching others that all lives and things of this world are one,

then, the results of that will become virtue and merit

that transcends any conception of virtue and merit.

"Why, Subhuti?

Because in doing this,

the one mind of all buddhas,

this supreme, bright, utterly true functioning of one mind,

which is expressed in all the sutras,

becomes one with you,

and with this,

the benefits of this nondual functioning of one mind

spread far and wide.

"Subhuti,

in short,

this great nondual functioning of one mind,

which ultimately can't even be called 'truth' or 'one mind,'

is every moment of our daily lives."

09 / 일체 상相이 상이 아님이니

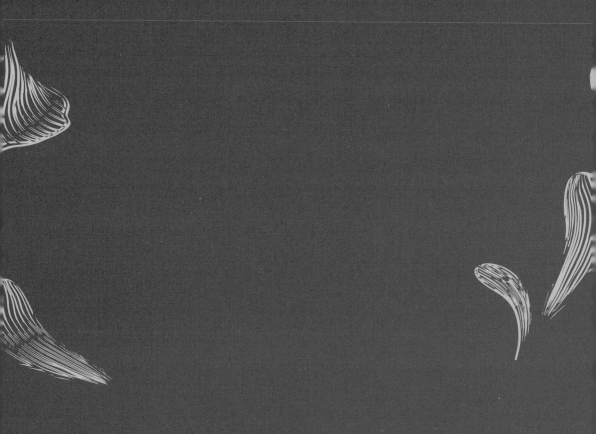

Chapter 9

What you see isn't what you are seeing

수보리야, 어떻게 생각하느냐.

오원의 한마음은 시공을 초월하여

생과 사에 얽매이지 않고

색色에 물들지 않는 마음을 내되

내가 생과 사도 없고

시간과 공간도 모든 색깔도 없는 뜻을

얻었다고 하겠는가?

" **S**ubhuti,
what do you think?

One mind,

where all energies are connected and work together as one,

unconstrained by time and space,

is never trapped by birth and death,

and gives rise to intentions unstained

by anything of the material world.

In the midst of this,

do you think that I have attained a state

free of discriminations between birth and death,

time and space, shapes and characteristics,

and divisions and categories?"

아니옵니다, 세존이시여.

무슨 까닭인가 하면

생사도 색깔도 시간도 없는 뜻이 흐른다 하지만

들고 나는 바가 없으니

색성향미촉법^{色聲香味觸法}도 있다 없다 함이 없으므로

이를 이름하여 수다원이라 합니다.

Subhuti answered,

"No, World-honored One.

Life and death, shapes and characteristics,

time and space are all manifesting together

as part of one flowing whole,

yet their appearance and disappearance,

their arising and ceasing fundamentally do not exist.

Thus, it can't be truly said that form, sounds, smells,

flavors, sensations, and thoughts exist or don't exist.

Someone who has sensed this is called a 'Stream Enterer.'"

수보리야, 어떻게 생각하느냐

사다함이 능히 이런 마음을 내되

내가 사다함과를 얻었다 하겠는가?

수보리가 말씀드리되

아니옵니다, 세존이시여.

왜냐하면 사다함은 이름일 뿐

산울림과 같은 고로

실은 가고 옴이 없으므로

이를 이름하여 사다함이라 합니다.

수보리야, 어떻게 생각하느냐

아나함이 능히 이런 생각을 내되

내가 아나함과를 얻었다고 하겠느냐?

"Subhuti, consider this:

Even though a Once-returner[14]

is capable of functioning as one with this whole,

does such a being think,

'I have attained the level of a Once-returner'?"

Subhuti answered,

"No, World-honored One,

because 'Once-returner' is just a label.

They are like an echo in the mountains,

that we label 'Once-returner.'

But in fact, there is no leaving or returning."

[14]
Once-returner:
Traditionally, this
describes someone
who needs to be reborn
one more time in order
to attain complete
enlightenment. Similarly,
a Non-returner is
traditionally someone
who has freed themselves
from the bonds of karma
such that they will not be
compelled into further
rebirths in the realms of
desire.

"Subhuti, consider this:

Could someone already freely functioning as a Non-returner,

think, 'I have attained the level of a Non-returner'?"

수보리가 말씀드리되

아니옵니다, 세존이시여.

왜냐하면 아나함은 이름일 뿐

마음은 체가 없어 가고 옴이 없으므로

실은 오고 감을 함이 없이 하는 까닭에

이름하여 아나함이라 합니다.

수보리야, 어떻게 생각하느냐

아라한이 능히 이런 생각을 하되

내가 아라한도를 얻었다 하겠느냐?

Subhuti answered,

"No, World-honored One,

because 'Non-returner' is just a convenient label.

Mind, of course, has no physical substance,

so there is nothing that would go or return.

Thus, such a being is able to freely manifest

throughout the world,

without any instant of arriving or leaving,

responding as one with the circumstances,

without the least trace of a dualistic 'I did,' or 'I will.'

Such a being is called a 'Non-returner.'"

"Subhuti, consider this:

Could an Arhat,

having fully experienced the depths of all

of these different aspects,

think, 'I have attained the way of an Arhat'?"

수보리가 말씀드리되

아니옵니다, 세존이시여.

왜냐하면 아라한이란 아라한이 아닌 까닭입니다.

세존이시여,

만약 아라한이 자기가 아라한도를 얻었다고 한다면

이는 곧 무명에서 벗어나지 못한 까닭에

일체 상에 집착하는 것입니다.

세존이시여,

부처님께서 말씀하시기를

수도자인 제가 내면의 자생중생들과

둘이 아닌 무심 삼매三昧를 얻은 사람 중에

제일이라 하시니

Subhuti answered,

"No, World-honored One.

For, one who has fully awakened,

understands there is no fixed aspect to be called 'Arhat.'

"Further,

if an Arhat should say that they've attained

the level of an Arhat,

then they are still trapped in ignorance,

and everything they do is subtly permeated by dualistic thinking.

"World-honored One,

you have said that,

I am the foremost among your disciples who have attained

the samadhi free of 'I,'

where oneself and all inner lives are one.

This seems like you are saying that I am the foremost Arhat,

일체 욕심을 떠난 제일의 아라한이라 하심인데

세존이시여,

저의 마음은 그렇지 않습니다.

그런 생각을 하지 않습니다.

모든 욕심에서 벗어나 둘 아닌 무심 도리를 얻었다 할지라도

아라한이라 이름을 세울 게 없습니다.

who has abandoned even the subtle forms of grasping[15]

and attained the nondual truth.

However,

I do not feel this way,

nor do I think this way.

Even if I had abandoned all forms of grasping

and attained the nondual truth that's free of 'I,'

there would still be nothing to call 'Arhat.'

15
Subtle forms of grasping:
The nuance here is the
desire or clinging to ideas
of doing positive things,
such as saving people.
So, although they have
moved beyond desires
such as lust and greed,
there is still a sense of
desire to do "good" things.

세존이시여,

제가 이런 생각을 해보되

내가 아라한도를 얻었다 한다면

세존께서는,

수보리는 아란나행을 세우는 자라고

말씀하지 않으셨으려니와

수보리가 실로 행하는 바가 없으므로

수보리는 아란나행을

함이 없이 하는 자라고 이름하셨을 것입니다.

"World-honored One,

I think that if I had truly attained this state,

then, instead of saying,

'Subhuti works hard at being

an excellent forest dweller,'[16]

you would have said,

'Subhuti is free of all ideas of doing or dwelling,

thus he is one who,

although living as a 'forest dweller,'

does so while becoming one with everything,

free of thoughts of 'doing,' or 'saving.'"

16
Forest dweller: A forest
would have been filled
with biting insects,
wild animals, bandits,
and limited food. Thus,
a "forest dweller" is
someone who lives in the
midst of that, unstained
and unshaken, responding
wisely to it all. This
is a metaphor for the
enlightened being who
lives in the world and
takes care of things ably
and with equanimity.

10 / 둘 아닌 공심, 즉 한자리인 것이니

Chapter 10

This nondual mind, which is everything working together as one

부처님께서 수보리에게 이르시되

어떻게 생각하느냐

공체共體 공심共心이 밝아

어제 오늘이 없는 회상에서

법을 얻은 바 있다고 하겠느냐?

아니옵니다, 세존이시여.

여래께서 한마음 도량

밝은 공심불 회상에 계실 때

공용共用의 법을 실로 얻은 바가 없습니다.

The Buddha asked Subhuti,

"In becoming aware of this great whole

that is the entire universe[17] working together as one,

where there is no 'yesterday' or 'today,'

do you think that I have attained something?"

"No, World-honored One.

When you experienced this great seat of wisdom,

one mind,

this bright light of all minds

functioning together as one,

this 'functioning together,'

was, in the truest sense,

not something you gained."

17
Universe: In Buddhism,
"universe" encompasses
multiple dimensions,
realms, parallel universes,
universes of the past and
future, and so forth.

수보리야, 어떻게 생각하느냐

보살이 불바퀴를 스스로

둘이 아니게 다스린다고 하겠느냐?

아니옵니다, 세존이시여.

왜냐하면 공생共生의 마음자리를 장엄이라 하는 것은

곧 마음자리가 아니고

그 이름이 마음자리이기 때문입니다.

그러므로 수보리야,

모든 보살마하살은 함이 없이 함으로써

진실한 마음을 낼지니

"Subhuti,

does it seem to you that bodhisattvas

take this great whole

that is everything working as one

and nondually control and direct it?"

"No, World-honored One,

in its functioning as one,

this wondrous working together of all lives and minds

encompasses all things naturally and automatically.

Words cannot touch upon this essence,

but for the sake of teaching,

we describe it as 'nondual mind.'"

"Thus, Subhuti,

the great bodhisattvas

are the functioning of all things together as one,

and their inconceivable guidance and help

arises naturally from this functioning of the whole.

물질에만 치우친 마음을 내지 말 것이며,

성향미촉법도 없는 까닭에 고정된 마음을 내지 말 것이며,

고정된 바 없이, 한 바 없이 마음을 낼지니라.

수보리야,

어떤 사람의 몸이 우주만 하다면

어떻게 생각하느냐

그 몸이 크다고 하겠느냐?

수보리가 말씀드리되

매우 큽니다, 세존이시여.

왜냐하면 둘 아닌 자아 부처님께서는

몸 아닌 것을 이름하여 큰 몸이라 하신 까닭입니다.

So do not get caught up in intentions and thoughts

that are skewed towards the material.

Do not give rise to fixed views or opinions,

for all things perceived through the five senses are fleeting,

and leave nothing behind.

Instead, thoroughly entrust everything inwardly,

and function from one mind,

free of all fixed views,

free of ideas of having done something.

"Subhuti,

what would you think if someone's body

was as big as the universe?"

Subhuti answered,

"That would be a very large body indeed, World-honored One,

for this great body that you are speaking of

is the combined functioning

and manifestation of our foundation,

which is the entire universe."

11 / 무위공덕이 제일 높음이오니

Chapter 11

The virtue and merit that arises through the intangible, boundless functioning of one mind is unsurpassed

수보리야,

갠지스강의 헤아릴 수 없는 모래알처럼

갠지스강이 또 많다면 어떻게 생각하느냐

그리고 모든 갠지스강의 모래는

얼마나 많겠느냐?

수보리가 말씀드리되

매우 많습니다, 세존이시여.

오원에는 있다 없다 할 수 없는 뜻이 있거늘

그 모래 수이겠습니까.

"Subhuti,
if all the uncountable grains of sand in the Ganges River
were each another Ganges,
can you imagine how much sand there would be?"

Subhuti replied,
"The amount of sand would indeed be unimaginable.
But even those huge numbers
are nothing in the face of
this indivisible functioning of one mind,
this unimaginable, infinite functioning of all energies,
connecting and working together as one,
such that they cannot be said to exist or not exist."

수보리야,

내가 이제 말함이 없이 말을 네게 이르노니

만약 어떤 지혜로운 남녀가

몸과 마음에서 끝없는 칠보 보배가 저 모래 수같이

삼천대천세계에 가득 채웠으니

한마음의 꽉 찬 보배로 보시를 한다면,

얻을 공덕이 많다고 하겠느냐?

수보리가 말씀드리기를

많다고 말로써 다 이르오리까, 세존이시여.

"Subhuti,

let me now speak to you without words,

from mind to mind:

If wise men and women practice diligently,

filling the vast universe with the endless treasures

arising from their body and mind,

treasures as abundant as the sands of the Ganges,

and then use these treasures of one mind to help others,

the resulting virtue and merit

would be beyond imagining, wouldn't it?"

Subhuti spoke,

"Indeed, World-honored One,

words could never begin to describe it."

한마음의 부처님께서 수보리에게 이르시되

만약 지혜로운 남녀가

내면의 선과 경이 둘이 아니게

그 가운데서

사구게가 사구게가 아님을 받아 지니고

자타가 둘 아닌 도리를 위해 설한다면

칠보로 삼천대천세계를 가득 채운

보시의 복덕보다

공덕이 수승하리라.

As one mind, the Buddha continued,

"Likewise, if wise men and women,

having understood that this inner spiritual practice

and these teachings are not separate,

that these verses are not mere words,

and so work to thoroughly reflect upon them,

applying them to their lives,

if these wonderful people should then go forward

and teach this truth of nonduality,

teaching for the sake of helping all beings live in tune with it,

so that this world can truly function as a nondual whole,

then the virtue and merit of that

will outshine,

will surpass,

even the virtue and merit of offering an entire universe

filled with the treasures of one mind."

12 / 바르게 가르침을 존중함이니

Chapter 12

Correctly teaching these verses is recognized throughout all realms

그리고 수보리야,

어디서나 이 경을 설하되

사구게 등이 공했다는 여여함으로 돌려 설한다면

일체 세간의 만물만생의 마음이

한마음으로 공양하기를

부처 중생 둘 아닌 중용으로 할 것이거늘

남녀노소를 막론하고

부처님의 뜻과 가르침을

진실로 받아 읽고 외워 뜻을 익힌다면

"Subhuti,
teach this sutra to people everywhere,

and when you do so,

point them towards the underlying meaning,

the interconnected, flowing whole,

which ceaselessly changes and manifests every instant.

If you do this,

the minds of all lives and things throughout every realm

will all be sustained,

will all be nourished

through the sublime functioning of one mind,[18]

where buddhas and unenlightened beings are not two.

"If anyone,

old or young, male or female,

sincerely embraces these teachings,

reflecting upon them,

applying them to their life,

and observing their effects in action,

[18]
Sublime functioning of one mind: This is the functioning of all beings as an interconnected whole, giving and receiving whatever is needed, in accord with their capacity to absorb it and their ability to function as part of this great whole.

수보리야, 마땅히 알라.

이 사람은 내면으로 믿고

물러서지 않는 사람의 최상이며

제일의 희유한 법을 성취할 것이니

만약 둘 아니게 걸림 없는 경전이 있는 곳이라면

곧 부처님과

한마음으로 존경받는

제자가 계신 곳이 되리라.

then, Subhuti,

know this:

Such a person,

is a foremost practitioner,

one who continues forward,

entrusting everything to their foundation,

regardless of whatever difficulty they encounter,

and in so doing,

will attain the most rarefied states of awareness.

Wherever the truths of this sutra are being taught,

these teachings of the ceaselessly flowing whole,

then there,

together,

will be all buddhas,

as well as those practitioners

recognized and honored by the interconnected whole."

13 / 법답게 받아 지님이니

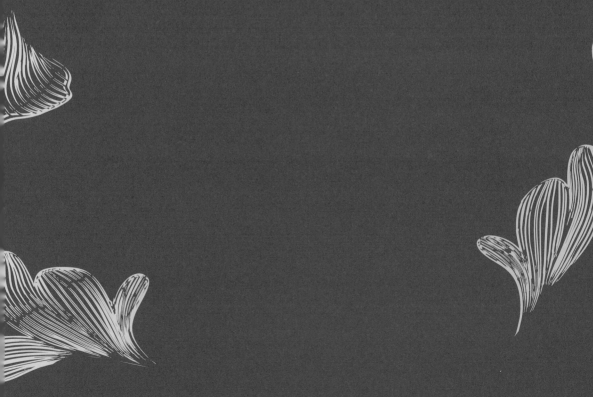

Chapter 13

Know that these teachings describe the underlying principles of how all things function, and deeply engrave them in your heart

13. 법답게 받아 지님이니

그때 수보리가 부처님께 사뢰었다.

세존이시여,

이 뜻의 경을

마땅히 무엇이라 이름할 것이며

저희들이 어떻게 받들어 지니오리까?

부처님께서 수보리에게 이르시되

이 경은

위없이 밝음에

한마음은 그대로 여여하여 영원할 것이며

일체 있는 걸 없는 줄 알고

없는 걸 있는 줄 안다면

그대로 영원한 줄 알리는 뜻이니

Subhuti then asked the Buddha,

"World-honored One,

what should these teachings be called,

and how can someone truly awaken to them

and live accordingly?"

The Buddha answered Subhuti,

"These teachings are about the unsurpassed brightness,

the supreme, awakened state,

so if you thoroughly realize that one mind,

the functioning of the whole as one,

is unceasing and eternal,

and that everything you perceive and all that is unseen

exist together nondually,

then you will see that these teachings are everlasting.

이러한 이름은 이름 없는 이름으로써

너희들은 한마음 깊은 속에

받들어 지녀야 하느니라.

그 까닭이 무엇인가, 수보리야.

부처가 설한 반야바라밀은

곧 반야바라밀이 아니고

그 이름이 반야바라밀이니라.

수보리야, 어떻게 생각하느냐

여래가 설한 바 법이 되겠느냐?

"Although many labels are used,

no names can ever truly describe these teachings,

you must work to know them from the depths of one mind

and then engrave them upon your heart

and apply them to daily life.

"For, Subhuti,

although all buddhas have taught

this 'supreme, perfect wisdom of emptiness,'

there is no such thing,

for, 'the supreme, perfect wisdom of emptiness' is just the label.

"Subhuti,

do you think that the teachings given by Tathagata

are the ultimate truth?"

수보리가 부처님께 말씀드리되

세존이시여, 여래께서는 설한 바가 없습니다.

수보리야, 어떻게 생각하느냐

삼천대천세계에 있는 모든 티끌이 많다고 생각하느냐?

수보리가 말씀드리되

매우 많습니다, 세존이시여.

수보리야,

모든 티끌을,

여래는 티끌이 세계와 둘이 아닌 것을 설하노니

그 이름이 티끌이며

여래는 세계가 세계가 아니라고 설하노니

그 이름이 세계이니라.

Subhuti answered the Buddha,

"World-honored One,

fundamentally there was never anything taught by Tathagata,

for Tathagata is the functioning that has no divisions."

"What do you think, Subhuti,

throughout all the worlds of the many realms,

would you say there is a lot of dust?"

"Yes, World-honored One, a vast amount."

"Subhuti,

Tathagata tells you that all of that dust

and all of those worlds are not two,

'Dust' is just a label,

'World' is just a label.

Tathagata tells you that even 'worlds'

as people think of them

do not exist.

Those are just labels.

수보리야, 어떻게 생각하느냐

삼십이상으로 여래를 볼 수 있겠느냐?

아니옵니다, 세존이시여.

삼십이상으로는 여래를 볼 수 없습니다.

왜냐하면

여래께서는 삼십이상은 곧 상이 아니라

이름이 삼십이상이라 하시기 때문입니다.

"Subhuti,

what do you think about the thirty-two marks of a buddha?[19]

Is it possible to recognize Tathagata through those?"

"No, no, World-honored One,

Tathagata cannot be perceived through the

thirty-two marks of a buddha,

for you have told us that those marks

don't truly describe Tathagata.

Those characteristics are just made-up labels."

19
**Thirty-two marks of
a buddha**: These were
physical characteristics
traditionally associated
with a great being, such as
long ears, slender fingers,
forty teeth, a pleasing
body odor, and so on.
On a deeper level, they
also represent abilities
such as the ability to hear
or know anything, the
ability to reach out and
influence things far away,
and so on. However,
even abilities such as
these don't actually
indicate awakening or an
enlightened being.

수보리야,

만약 어떤 지혜 있는 남녀가 있어서

일체 한마음의 나툼으로

천차만별의 모습과 마음이 화하여 나투며

둘이 아닌 보시를 하고,

또 어떤 사람이 있어서

이 경 가운데서 사구게가 따로 없이

내면의 밝은 마음을 지녀서

나와 남을 위해 둘 아니게 설한다면

그 공덕은 끝이 없을 것이니라.

"Subhuti,

if wise men and women should become one with one mind,

then the nondual aid they offer will transform and manifest

according to the shapes and levels of awareness

that are needed.

Unlike good karma or good fortune,

the virtue and merit of that will shine forever.

"Similarly, if someone,

awakens this utterly bright mind,

which inherently contains all the meanings of these verses,

and then, with this luminous mind,

teaches and guides others nondually,

so that oneself and all other beings benefit,

then, unlike good karma or good fortune,

the virtue and merit of that will shine forever."

14 / 상相을 떠나야 적멸함이니라

Chapter 14

Ultimate tranquility comes after leaving behind fixed ideas and views

그때 수보리가

둘이 아닌 경의 설하심을 듣고

깊이 그 뜻을 깨달아

과거 부父와 현재 자子가 상봉하여

눈물과 기쁨이 둘이 아닌 까닭에

부처님께 사뢰었다.

희유하십니다, 세존이시여.

부처님께서

정신계와 물질계가 둘이 아닌 깊은 경을 설하심이니

나 아닌 나가 과거사를 아는 바

혜안으로도 미처 이 같은 경과 선이 둘 아닌 말씀은

얻어듣지 못하였습니다.

Hearing these nondual teachings,
Subhuti deeply awakened.
The father and the son had met,
his true nature, which had guided him over eons,
and his present consciousness had combined.
With both tears and joy,[20]
Subhuti spoke to the Buddha:

20
Tears and joy: This was his joy at awakening and his sadness at realizing the depths of ignorance of sentient beings.

"How rare and amazing, World-honored One!

As you explained these deep teachings to me

of the nondual functioning

of the material and the spiritual as one incomparable whole,

I realized that even though I have the Wisdom Eye,

where the me that is not me

knows my lives far into the past,

never in any of those lives have I heard that

the teachings and inner spiritual practice[21]

are ultimately the same thing.

21
Teachings and inner spiritual practice: Because the material and the spiritual function together nondually, material based practices, such as studying the sutras, listening to teachings, and helping others to understand them, and spiritually based, inward practices, all ultimately lead to the same understanding of the functioning of this whole.

세존이시여,

만약 어떤 사람이 이 말씀을 듣고

신심을 내면

깊이 진실하게 내며

곧 실상의 근본을 얻으려니와

이 사람은 진정 제일의 공덕을

성취할 것을 믿겠습니다.

세존이시여,

이 실상이란 상이 아니기에,

이런 까닭에 여래께서는 실상이라 이름하셨습니다.

"World-honored One,

 I believe that anyone who hears your words

and gives rise to faith in their own nondual essence,

will find this faith growing in depth and sincerity,

and will perceive the foundation of reality.

Such people will, I believe, attain the greatest virtue and merit.

"World-honored One,

this reality, as I understand it, is not some limited,

incomplete aspect,

it is not something that fixed views can encompass.

Thus, Tathagata describes it as 'reality.'

세존이시여,

제가 이와 같은

공하여 그대로 여여한 경의 말씀을 듣고

믿어 알고 받아 지니기는 어렵지 않사오나

만약 미래 세상 후 현재 세상이 왔을 때에

그 어떤 중생이

이 경의 말씀을 얻어듣고 믿어 알고

미래를 돌아 현재 오늘에

그 경의 말씀을 내면에 받아 지니면

이 사람은 위없는 진실한 사람일 것입니다.

왜냐하면 이 사람은 아상이 없고

나다, 내가 했다, 내가 위대하다 하는 게 없기 때문입니다.

"World-honored One,

meeting you and having you explain to me

the nondual workings of the whole,

and how they are ceaselessly changing and manifesting,

it is not difficult to believe in them,

to understand them,

and to engrave them in my heart.

But in the far future,

in the ever-present 'now' that is always here,

if someone should happen to hear these teachings,

and has faith in them

engraving them in their heart,

and applying them throughout their daily life,

then they would, I believe,

be someone of unsurpassed sincerity and authenticity.

Such a person like this

would have to already be free of ideas of 'I,'

of 'me,' 'I did,' and 'I've achieved an exalted state.'

그 까닭이 무엇인가 하면

깨달으면 곧 아상이 상이 아니며

나다, 내가 했다, 내가 위대하다 하는 것이

곧 상이 아니기 때문입니다.

왜냐하면 일체 모든 상을 여읜 까닭에

모두가 부처라 이름하기 때문입니다.

부처님께서 수보리에게 이르시되

그렇다, 만약 어떤 사람이 이 경의 말씀을 듣고

일체 무심세계에서

놀라지 않고 두려워하거나 겁내지도 않으면

마땅히 알라,

이 사람의 마음은

더없이 밝고 맑음이니라.

"If someone awakens,

then even though they use words such as,

'I did,' 'I am,' or 'I'm unsurpassed,'

this 'I' comes from and describes

the workings of the whole as one.

For such a person has already left behind

all dualistic ideas and fixed views,

and so is called 'Buddha' by everyone far and near."

The Buddha replied to Subhuti,

"Indeed, Subhuti,

should someone, upon hearing these teachings,

enter the states free of dualistic discrimination

and be neither disturbed

nor apprehensive,

nor fearful,

then such a person's mind

would, indeed, be one of unsurpassed brightness and clarity.

왜냐하면 수보리야,

여래가 설하신 제일바라밀은

곧 제일바라밀이 아니요

그 이름이 제일바라밀이니라.

수보리야,

몸으로 고행을 하는 것도

여래는 몸으로 고행을 하는 것이 아니라고 설하신다.

그 이름이 고행한다는 것이니라.

왜냐하면 수보리야,

내가 나의 뿌리, 즉 자성왕에게

몸이 갈기갈기 찢기는 듯 고행을 했어도

그때에 나는 모든 상을 무심으로, 정신과 물질을 둘로 보지 않았으며

나다, 내가 했다, 내가 위대하다든가

그런 마음이 없었기 때문이다.

146

"Subhuti,

this great Paramita[22] that Tathagata has been speaking of

is not the 'great Paramita' that people think of,

for 'Paramita' is just a label.

"Subhuti,

the same is true for asceticism.

Tathagata is telling you now that asceticism

is not practiced through the body.

'Asceticism' is just how it appears from the outside.

"For, Subhuti,

even when it felt like my own root,

my inner king was tearing my body to pieces,

I was able to view everything from this deep place of one mind,

and see mind and matter as one functioning whole,

because I had absolutely no thoughts of 'I,'

of 'I did,' or 'I am superior.'

왜냐하면 나의 육신이 내면 부(父)의 채찍에

사지가 마디마디 찢기는 듯 아파도

만약에 모든 상이나 물질에 치우쳐

둘로 생각했다면

자기가 있기에 자기 탓인 줄 모르고

남을 원망하고 증오하며

미워하는 마음을 내었을 것이기 때문이다.

수보리야,

과거 현재 미래 없는 오백 세 동안

인욕을 내면에 돌려놓고 있었던 일을 생각하였느니라.

"When my flesh was being lashed

and urged forward

by my inner father,

when my body hurt so much

that it felt as if it was being torn limb from limb,

if I had been focused on the material aspect,

or thought that things existed apart from myself,

then I wouldn't have understood

that my presence is the source of everything

I experience.[23]

Instead, I would have fallen into resentment,

into hatred,

into despising.

"Subhuti,

even over the course of five hundred lifetimes,

where there was ultimately

no past, present, or future,

when I was already free from the view

that there was a 'me' that was doing things,

[23]
My presence is the source of what I experience: This is not simple blame, but rather the idea that our current state is the result of our actions, and thus our future state is also under our control. What we think of as ourselves is the combination of (1) our Buddha-nature, our foundation, which has guided us as we've evolved to this point. (2) All of the tangled up karmic affinity we've created as we've tried to evolve, including our missteps. (3) Our present consciousness or awareness, which is the result of both of these, and (4) our body.

The key point is that because we are the ultimate source of what we're experiencing, we also have the power to change our state. We have the ability to set things moving in a different direction, but as long as we attribute someone or something else with the power that got us here, we are denying ourselves the ability to move forward.

그때 세상에서도 아상이 없었고

인상 · 중생상 · 수자상도 없었느니라.

그러므로 수보리야,

깨달은 사람은 응당 일체, 일체 상을 떠나서

위없는 진실한 한마음으로

조건 없는 자비심을 낼지니

응당 모든 물질에 마음을 내지 말고

이론이나 냄새, 감촉, 법을 내면에 놓고

공한 마음이니,

free from the view of having achieved a certain level of
spiritual evolution,
free from the view of others existing as unawakened beings,
free from the view of being constrained by time or space,
I still, nonetheless,
had to return inwardly all of the suffering and hardships
I experienced in those times,
in those realms.

"Similarly, Subhuti,
those who have awakened,
must, as a matter of course,
leave behind all views and perceptions,
and give rise to unconditional compassion for all beings
through this unsurpassed one mind.
You must not get caught up in the material world,
and should instead take all smells, physical contact,
perceptions, and received knowledge
and return it inwardly.

고정된 바가 없으니

함이 없는 마음을 낼지니라.

마음은 찰나찰나 화하는데 머물 곳이 있으랴.

그러므로 부처님께서 말씀하시기를

깨달은 사람은 모든 물질에 탐이 없이

한마음 내어 보시하라.

수보리야,

깨달은 이는 일체 중생을 이익 되게 하기 위해

응신으로 화하여 나투며 보시하느니라.

You have to give rise to thoughts as one mind,

free of all discriminations,

for here everything functions as one whole,

ceaselessly flowing and changing.

In this endlessly flowing and transforming whole,

could there be any part of it that stands still?"

The Buddha continued,

"Thus, those who have awakened,

must, without clinging to anything in the world,

help others as one mind.

"Subhuti,

for the sake of all beings far and wide,

those who have awakened

should manifest through this one mind,

according to circumstances and needs.

여래가 설하신 일체 모든 상이 곧 상이 아니며

또한 일체 중생이라고 설함도,

곧 중생이 아닌 것이다 함도

부처 중생이 둘이 아닌 까닭이니라.

수보리야,

여래는 진실한 말을 하는 자이며

말이 아닌 진실한 말을 하는 자이며

거짓 없이 말하는 자이며

거짓 아닌 참을 말하는 자이며

말 아닌 말을 하지 않는 자이다.

"All of the things that Tathagata has taught

are not the fixed ideas that people took away with them.

Not the ideas they thought that Tathagata said

about unenlightened beings,

nor what they thought Tathagata said about awakened beings.

For unenlightened beings and buddhas are not two.

"Subhuti,

Tathagata only ever speaks the truth,

Tathagata only ever speaks with the utmost sincerity,

Tathagata never speaks with any falseness,

Tathagata speaks without the least deceptiveness,

Tathagata never speaks from dualistic discriminations or

fixed ideas.

수보리야,

여래가 얻은 법은

있는 것도 없고 없는 것도 없느니라.

수보리야,

만약 깨달은 사람의 마음이

법에 고정된 관념으로 보시한다 하면

사람이 캄캄한 통 속에서 보지 못함과 같고

만약 깨달은 사람의 마음이

걸림 없이 법의 보시행을 하면

마치 사람이 심안이 밝아서

일체를 보는 사이 없이 보는 것과 같느니라.

"Subhuti,

the truth known to Tathagata

is not something that exists or doesn't exist.

"Subhuti,

should an awakened person try to give aid and compassion

while still dwelling in a fixed sense of the truth,

then it would be as if they were trapped in a dark barrel,

unable to see anything,

unable to correctly perceive anything.

However,

if an awakened mind offers the aid and compassion

of one mind while unhindered by anything,

then they would be like someone whose inner eye is bright,

who truly perceives everything that's happening

in all the realms around them.

수보리야,

미래에 오는 현재 세상에

어떤 남성과 여성이

부처님께서 설하신 경을

받아 지니고 읽고 믿으면,

곧 일체 만물만생의 한마음 속에

부처님의 지혜로써 마음이 통하는 사람은

우주법계에서도 보는 것도 말하는 것도 마음도

일체 통한 이런 사람은

한량없고 끝없는 공덕을 성취하게 되리라.

"Subhuti,

in the far future, in this ever-present now,

those men and women

who embrace these teachings of the Buddha,

studying them and having faith in them,

that is to say,

those men and women who become aware of

the Buddha-wisdom found within the one mind

of all lives and things,

and through that, are able to engage with others,

these men and women who see, speak, and think

as one with everything in the Dharma realms,

will all come to attain unimaginable,

inconceivable virtue and merit."

15 /
선과 경을 둘이 아니게 지닌 공덕은 자유로워서

Chapter 15

The virtue and merit that comes from embracing the teachings and inner spiritual practice as one is beyond imagining and reaches everywhere

수보리야,

만약 어떤 지혜있는 남녀가 있어

아침나절에 찰나에

천백억화신이 응신으로 나투며 자비 보시하고

낮밤이 없이 갠지스강 모래 수같이

원심에서 천차만별의 모습으로 응신 되어 나투며 보시하고,

아침 저녁에도 원심에서 갠지스강 모래 수같이

응신으로 화하여 나투며 보시하였네.

"Subhuti,
there are men and women,
who, in the mornings,
help people unconditionally by manifesting into the world
with a thousand million different forms.
Day and night,
they give aid, responding from their complete, inherent mind,
manifesting with more different shapes
than there are sands of the Ganges.
At all hours of the day,
they've given immeasurable help and compassion
by responding from this complete, inherent mind,
transforming and manifesting with more shapes
than there are sands of the Ganges.

이와 같이 아침 저녁 점심

둘이 아닌

주장심의 한마음으로

헤아릴 수 없이 백천만억 겁을

천차만별의 모습으로 나투어 응신으로서 보시하였으니

한마음의 응신의 보시는 끝이 없어라.

만약 어떤 사람이

선과 경을 둘이 아니게 지니고 듣고

믿는 마음으로 배척하지 않으면

그 공덕이 끝 간 데 없으리라.

"Determined to help other beings,

they have given aid and compassion

in every moment of the day

over uncountable billions of eons,

by responding and manifesting

as one mind,

with millions of different shapes and forms.

The help that arises from this nondual oneness

is utterly without limits.

"Similarly, should someone embrace this inner spiritual practice

and the teachings as one,

such that they, as their fundamental essence,

directly teach themselves,

if they then have faith in this and don't turn away from it,

the virtue and merit of that will be truly endless.

진실한 마음으로 베껴 쓰고 받아 지녀 읽고

내면에 몰락 놓고 감사히 생각하면서

남을 위해 알아듣게 설명해 줌에

이 세상이 공심인 줄 알리라.

수보리야, 요약해서 말할진대

이 경은

마음 떠난 적 없는, 즉 둘이 아닌 까닭에

생각할 수도 없으며 잴 수도 없는

한없는 공덕이 있느니라.

When they sincerely explore these teachings,

pondering their implications

while completely entrusting everything that happens

inwardly, with gratitude,

then, as they try to help others understand

each according to their ability and capacity,

those people, too,

will come to realize that this entire world

functions as one, nondual whole.

"Subhuti,

to summarize:

Because the essence of these teachings is nonduality,

in which everything is ceaselessly functioning together

as one mind,

the virtue and merit of helping others perceive this

is beyond imagining,

cannot be measured,

and is truly without limit.

여래는 대승에 발심한 자를 위해

선과 경이 둘 아닌 설법을 하시며

최상승에 발심한 자를 위해 설하시느니

어떤 사람이

공생共生 · 공용共用 · 공체共體 · 공식共食인 도리를

내면에 지니고 읽어서

널리 사람들을 위해 설한다면

여래는 이 사람들을 모두 알며 모두를 보나니

모두들 헤아릴 수 없고 잴 수도 없고

말할 수도 없고 끝이 없고

생각할 수 없는 공덕을 성취하게 되리라.

"For those who wish to awaken

so that they can help other beings trapped in suffering,

for those who wish to attain the deepest freedom of enlightenment,

Tathagata has taught the workings of the nondual whole,

in which spiritual practice and the teachings

are ultimately the same.

Should such people embrace the deep truth

that all beings have this foundation, and through it,

all lives and bodies are connected as one,

working together as one, freely giving and receiving all things,

should they make this truth their own

and then teach it to people far and wide,

so that others, too, can know this for themselves,

they will be known to Tathagata,

they will be watched over by Tathagata.

They will all achieve fathomless,

measureless,

inexpressible,

unimaginable,

unending,

virtue and merit.

이런 사람들은

곧 여래의 위없는 진실한 한마음을 깨우친 마음과

둘 아닌 한마음으로 밝았느니라.

왜냐하면 수보리야,

작은 법을 좋아하는 자는

나의 마음으로부터

일거일동 집착하게 되므로

무명 굴레를 벗어나지 못하느니

곧 선과 경을 둘 아닌 진실한 마음으로

읽고 받아 지녀서 남을 위해 해설해 주면

고^苦에서 벗어나게 되느니 그 공덕이 크니라.

"People like this,

who are aware of the peerless, utterly profound,

awakened one mind that is the essence of Tathagata,

glow with the light of this nondual one mind.

"Why is there such virtue and merit, Subhuti?

Because those people who are still dwelling in narrow views

tend to cling to every little thing,

so it's hard for them to take even one step forward,

much less to escape from the harness of ignorance.

Thus, when you engage in spiritual practice as one mind,

when you study the teachings as one mind,

seeing into their marrow and understanding their essence,

and applying them throughout the world of your daily life,

if you then share what you've learned

with those who are still trapped,

teaching them according to their ability to understand,

they will be able to free themselves from the wheel of suffering.

The virtue and merit of this will be incredible.

수보리야,

어느 곳이든,

일체 둘이 아닌 경이 있는 곳이라면

일체 세간 천인^{天人}들의 마음이 밝아서

응당 한마음의 재식 공양을 하리라.

마땅히 알라.

곧 내 마음 근본이 탑이 됨이라.

"Subhuti,

in any realm or era with these nondual teachings,

there are wonderful beings

who will thus brighten their minds,

and, as a matter of course,

will share the nectar of one mind far and wide.

Know that if you brighten your mind like this,

your fundamental mind

will become a pagoda.[24]

24
Pagoda: In one sense, pagodas are monuments to the Buddha and great practitioners, but they can also be thought of as a place where the essence of Buddha still exists. Further, Seon Master Daehaeng has described a true pagoda as something that can communicate with the middle, higher, and lower realms, and even compared this functioning to that of an antenna.

마음의 근본이 탑이라면

공경을 갖추어

고정됨이 없이 마음이 나투어 돌며

아름다운 마음으로 향기로운 마음 내어

만물만생에게 자비의 마음을 뿌리리라.

"If your fundamental mind becomes such a pagoda,

connecting to all beings,

caring for and respecting them,

it will flow and manifest freely,

according to beings' needs and their ability to understand.

With such a beautiful heart,

the fragrant intentions you give rise to

will spread loving help far and wide,

to beings of every shape and kind."

16 /
능히 이러하다면 업장 굴레에서 벗어나리라

Chapter 16

*Anyone who can thoroughly do this will free themselves
from the chains of karma*

다시 수보리야,

어떤 지혜로운 남녀가

공한 진리의 경을 독송하여도

남에게서 갖은 수모를 다 받는다 하면

이 사람은

전생의 죄업으로 응당 악도에 떨어질 것이나

이 세상에서 갖은 수모를 받는 까닭에

선세의 죄업이 곧 소멸되리라.

마땅히 위없는 진실한 깨달음을 얻으리라.

"Subhuti,
among those women and men
who are diligently putting into practice
these teachings of flowing emptiness,
there are some who, nonetheless,
experience humiliation and abuse at the hands of others.
However, know that this is due to the karma of past lives,
which would otherwise have caused them to fall into evil paths.
Further, because they have experienced those things
here, now,
and can apply these teachings to their hardships,
that harmful karma from generations past
will soon fade away.
Doing so, such practitioners will,
without a doubt,
attain unsurpassed, utterly profound enlightenment.

수보리야,

내가 과거 아닌 과거에

불바퀴에서 생각해 보니

밝은 마음이

어제 오늘 없는 사무사유四無四有 둘이 아니어서

사천만억 나유타의 일체 부처님의 한마음이

내 마음과 둘이 아니게 통하여 만나서

모두 다 둥근 떡으로

삼세를 공양하여도

줄지 않는 공양을 베풀어 영원하리라.

"Subhuti,

in the past that isn't past,

from the depths of the great circling energy,

I perceived that in this bright mind,

there are no discriminations,

that all material realms and all non-material realms

work together as one,

without 'yesterday' or 'today,'

thus my mind is one with,

communicates with,

the one mind of all buddhas,

of every buddha,

of a hundred trillion buddhas,

and as this nondual one mind,

this whole has offered sustenance,

the completeness of one mind,

to every being throughout the past, present, and future.

This energy of one mind never diminishes,

and shines throughout all eternity.

만약 어떤 사람이 있어 미래를 지나

오늘 세상에 말세가 와도

말세는 그 이름일 뿐이라,

능히 선과 경을 둘이 아니게 내면에 지니고

독송하되 함이 없이 한다면

얻은 바 없이 공덕이 되리라.

"Thus, if someone, passing through the future,

should arrive at a 'today' that is an utterly degenerate age,

a World-Ending Age,

know that even those are just words and labels.

If such a person should treasure this nondual energy,

trying to rely upon their inherent foundation,

as well as learning from the teachings,

seeing both of these paths as one,

engraving the essence of these in their heart

and reflecting upon it,

reciting these teachings as one mind,

letting go of all discriminations,

then, their actions, just as they are,

will all be virtue and merit.

내가 여러 부처님께

공양한 바 없이 공양을 올렸기에

공덕 아닌 공덕이라

공양한 바 없기에

백분의 일에 못 미침도 없고

천만억분의 일에 못 미침도 없음이니

숫자로 비유할 수 없어서 없다고 하는 까닭이니라.

"Because I freely shared the energy of this nondual mind

while one with it,

it became an offering to all buddhas.

Because it was done as one mind,

there was no 'giving,'

thus those offerings became virtue and merit

that was vastly beyond any conceptions of virtue and merit.

And so, this offering lacked nothing.

Not even one part of a hundred,

not even one part of a thousand million.

Numbers cannot begin to describe this offering,

so when asked, I just say,

'Nothing was given, and nothing was received.'

수보리야,

만약 지혜로운 남녀가 이후 말세에

이 경을 내면에 새겨 놓아

둘 아니게 공하였음을 안다면

깨우침에 한마음으로 내가 설하여도

혹 어떤 사람은 못 믿는 마음이 일어

의심하고 믿지 않으리니

수보리야, 마땅히 알라.

심안경설은 생각으로 의논할 수 없고

모든 과보도 가히 생각으로 헤아릴 수 없나니라.

"Subhuti,

should men and women,

in some later, degenerate age,

engrave these teachings in their hearts,

and so come to know this nondual emptiness,

and then, were I, as one mind,

to speak through such men and women,

through this awakened one mind,

and tell people about the nature of this nondual mind

and its functioning,

there might be those who wouldn't believe it,

who would doubt it.

"But know this, Subhuti,

these teachings have arisen from this nondual one mind,

and so cannot be known through thoughts and theories.

Nor can thoughts fathom

what realizing this essence brings to fruition,

or the terrible results of denying or ignoring

this underlying truth of nondual emptiness."

17 / 끝 간 데 없이 내가 없음이라

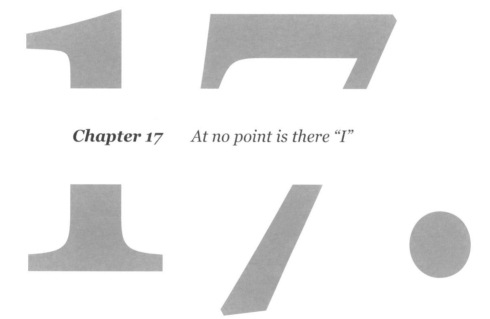

Chapter 17   *At no point is there "I"*

그때 수보리가 부처님께 사뢰었다.

세존이시여,

지혜로운 남녀가

위없는 진실한 한마음을 깨우쳐

걸림 없이 다스리니

어떻게 행하며

어떻게 그 마음을 항복받으오리까?

부처님께서 이르시되

지혜로운 남녀가

위없는 진실한 한마음을 깨우쳐

걸림 없이 일체를 다스려서

마땅히 이와 같이 공심을 내게 하리라.

At that time,
Subhuti asked the Buddha,

"World-honored One,

when men and women

awaken to this utterly profound, unsurpassed one mind,

and can respond free of dualistic views and attachments,

how should they help others?

How can they cause the unenlightened states of minds

they encounter to submit to and follow this one mind?"

The Buddha replied,

"If men and women awaken to this unsurpassed one mind,

and are able to respond fully like this,

then, naturally, all buddhas will be there together with them,

one with them,

supporting their efforts to help unenlightened beings.

The minds of those beings, too,

will begin to move in tune with one mind.

내가 응당 일체 중생을

업의 굴레에서 법에 의해

벗어나게 할 것이나

일체 중생 자신들이 벗어나게 해야

이후에도 고에서 벗어나리라.

실은 멸하게 해 주어도 자신이 모르면

세세생생 고의 굴레에서 벗어날 수 없나니라.

Although I, as the manifestation of one mind,

can, of course,

save unenlightened beings from the suffering

they are currently trapped in due to the chains of karma,

if they are to be free of future suffering,

they must learn to become one with this fundamental mind

so that they have the ability to free themselves.

"The fact is, even though I dissolve their present suffering,

if they don't know how to do this for themselves,

then, life after life,

they will continue to fall back into the bondage of suffering.

왜냐하면 수보리야,

만약 보살이

일체 나라는 상을 놓지 않고 둘로 본다면

보살이 아니니

내가 모든 상에서 벗어나야

삼세의 굴레에서 벗어나야

곧 보살이 아님을 알 수 있는 깨달음이니라.

까닭이 무엇인가, 수보리야.

실로 법이 있어서

뜻에 의해 위없는 진실한 한마음을 내어

중생을 다 건졌다 해도 건진 게 없느니라.

"In the same way, Subhuti,

if even a bodhisattva

carries around fixed views of themself

or subtly sees others as existing apart from themself,

then they cannot function as a bodhisattva.

You have to free yourself from fixed views and ideas,

you have to transcend the shackles of time,

then you can become one with everything,

and will truly know that there are no separate

unenlightened beings or bodhisattvas.

"For, Subhuti,

even having awakened

and saved unenlightened beings of all kinds,

such saving is done by becoming one with everything,

as this unsurpassed one mind,

so there is no separate being that's saved.

수보리야, 생각이 어떠하냐

여래가 한마음 불바퀴 속에서

위없는 진실의 한마음을 깨우친 법이 있겠느냐?

아니옵니다, 세존이시여.

제가 부처님께서 설하신 바 뜻을 알기로는

부처님께서는

한마음 불바퀴 처소에서

위없는 진실한 한마음을 깨우친 법이 있지 않습니다.

부처님께서 말씀하시되

함이 없이 하는 까닭이니라.

수보리야,

실로 법이 따로 있어

여래가 위없는 진실한 한마음을 깨우쳐

얻은 바가 아니니라.

"Subhuti,

in the midst of the great flowing and interconnecting energy

of one mind,

is there a truth of this profound

one mind that Tathagata awoke to?"

"No, World-honored One,

if I understand what you have taught,

then, in the great interconnecting energy of one mind,

there is no separate truth of this utterly profound

one mind to discover."

The Buddha replied,

"This is because everything is working as one whole.

Subhuti,

there is no separate truth for Tathagata to have attained

because Tathagata is itself this utterly profound,

unsurpassed one mind,

this great flowing and interconnecting energy of the whole.

수보리야,

만약 법이 있어

여래가 위없는 진실한 한마음의 도리를

깨우쳐 얻을진댄

한마음 불바퀴 속에서

나에게 수기하면서

　"너는 다음 세에 마땅히 부처를 이루리니

　명호를 석가모니로 하라."

그러나 이는 함이 없이 하신 말씀이니

실로 법이 아닌 법이라,

위없는 진실한 한마음의 깨달음은

얻은 것이 아니므로 얻은 것이니라.

"However, Subhuti,

if it could be said there was a truth that was attained,

it was the peerless functioning of one mind.

Thus, it came to be that this great flowing energy of one mind,

gave rise to the following intention:

In the next world cycle,

you will become a buddha.

There you will be called

'The Sage of the Shakyas.' [25]

25
Sage of the Shakyas:
This is the literal meaning
of "Shakyamuni."

"It was from this utter wholeness that this intention arose,

and having arisen from this one mind,

it manifested and functioned throughout all realms.

In this wholeness,

awakening to the peerless functioning of one mind

is not some separate thing that can be attained,

but, in a sense, it can also be said that

only after realizing that there was nothing separate to attain,

is it possible to awaken to the peerless functioning

of one mind.

이런 까닭에 연등불께서

나에게 수기를 주며 말씀하여 이르되

　"너와 나와 둘이 아니게

　내세에 마땅히 부처를 이뤄

　호를 석가모니로 하리라." 하신 것이다.

무슨 까닭이냐 하면

여래란

일체 만물만생의 법이

둘이 아닌 한마음으로 여여하게 돈다는 뜻이라.

"Having thus arisen from the whole in this way,

the Buddha known as 'Light Giver,'

gave voice to this intention, saying:

> *In the next world cycle*
>
> *you will become one with this whole,*
>
> *where you and I are one.*
>
> *There, you shall become a buddha*
>
> *and will be known as 'Shakyamuni.'*

"How was all of this possible?

Because what is called Tathagata

is the working together of all things, seen and unseen,

together as one,

flowing as one.

만약 어떤 사람이

여래께서 위없는 진실한 한마음을 깨달았을 때

깨달음을 얻었다고 말하겠느냐?

수보리야,

실로 법이 있어

부처가 위없는 법을 얻은 것이 아니니라.

수보리야,

여래인 까닭에 얻은 바 없느니라.

위없는 진실한 한마음의 깨달음 가운데에

깨달았다 함도 없고

깨닫지 않음도 없느니라.

그런고로 둘이 아닌 여래가 설하는 일체 법이,

우주 만물만생 일체가 다 불법佛法이니라.

"So, would it make sense if someone said,

'When Tathagata awoke to this peerless one mind,

Tathagata gained enlightenment'?

"Subhuti,

this supreme truth of one mind that the Buddha awoke to

was ultimately never anything separate.

"Subhuti,

because Tathagata is one mind,

there is nothing to be gained.

In the midst of this utterly profound,

peerless enlightenment of one mind,

there is nothing to call 'awakened' or 'unawakened.'

Therefore,

Tathagata, which is one with everything,

teaches that all lives and things throughout the universe

function together nondually,

as one whole.

수보리야,

말한 바 일체 법이라는 것은

곧 일체 법이 공하였으므로

이름하여 일체 법이니라.

수보리야, 비유하건대

사람 몸속에 자생중생들이

헤아릴 수 없이 많고 많은 것과 같느니라.

"Subhuti,

everything Tathagata has spoken to you about the existence

and functioning of all lives and things,

is the deepest truth,

for it is the flowing and working together of all things

as one whole.

"Subhuti,

the existence and functioning of all lives and things

is like that of the unenlightened beings that make up your body:

They too function as one nondual whole,

and exist in numbers beyond counting."

수보리가 말씀드리기를

세존이시여,

일체가 뭉친 하나이신 여래께서 설한

안과 밖이 없는 사람 몸의 장대함도

고정됨이 없이 찰나찰나 화하는 까닭에

큰 몸이라 이름함이옵니다.

수보리야,

보살도 이와 같느니라.

만약 말을 하되

내가 무량 중생을

모든 고에서 벗어나게 한다 하면

곧 보살이라 이름할 수 없느니라.

Subhuti replied,

"World-honored One,

because this body, too,

is a collection of lives

ceaselessly functioning as one,

with no divisions of inside or outside,

transforming and evolving every instant,

Tathagata, which is one with everything,

calls this magnificent functioning,

'the great all-pervading body.'"

"Subhuti,

know that bodhisattvas, too,

function exactly like this.

Thus, if someone were to say,

'I am able to save uncountable beings

from every kind of suffering,'

it would be clear that they could not function

as one with everything.

왜냐하면 수보리야,

실로 법이 법이 아닌 까닭에

보살이라 이름하지 않기 때문이니라.

그러므로 부처님이 설하되

일체 법은 마음도 없고 나도 없고

중생도 없고 수자壽者도 없다 하느니라.

수보리야,

만약 보살이 생각하여 말을 하되

내가 깨우쳤다, 내가 불국토를 장엄한다 하면

보살이라 이름할 수 없느니라.

"Why, Subhuti?

Because although the beings you encounter

and the things you experience exist,

their essence isn't how you perceive it.

Everything functions as part of one

interconnected, flowing whole.

This is why fully awakened ones

teach that in this great, flowing oneness,

there is no 'mind,'

no 'I,' no 'unenlightened beings,'

nor the constrained lifespan that beings appear to have.

"Subhuti,

should a bodhisattva think,

even with sincerity and humility,

'I have awakened,'

or, 'my actions are causing this Buddha Land to flourish,'

then they cannot fulfill the true functioning of a bodhisattva.

무슨 까닭인가?

여래가 설한 불국토를 장엄함이란

곧 장엄이 아니라

일체 공한 까닭에

그 이름이 장엄이니라.

수보리야,

만약 보살이

무아의 법을 통달한 자라면

일체 한마음의 여래는

참다운 보살이라,

이름하여 큰 보살이라 하느니라.

"Why?

What Tathagata calls

the flourishing of the Buddha's Land

is not caused by adding something,

but rather by the working together of everything as one whole.

Thus, it is called, 'flourishing.'

"Subhuti,

if a bodhisattva

has thoroughly mastered the depths of non-self,

of becoming one with everything,

then Tathagata,

this great one mind,

calls them a true bodhisattva,

a great bodhisattva."

18 / 일체 만물만생을 둘 아니게 봄이니

Chapter 18

Seeing absolutely everything nondually

수보리야, 어떻게 생각하느냐

여래가 육안肉眼이 있느냐?

그렇습니다, 세존이시여

여래는 심안心眼이 있습니다.

수보리야, 어떻게 생각하느냐

여래에 천안天眼이 있겠느냐?

그렇습니다, 세존이시여

여래는 일체 천안天眼이 있습니다.

수보리야, 어떻게 생각하느냐

여래에 혜안慧眼이 있겠느냐?

"Subhuti, think about this:
Does Tathagata have eyes?"

"Yes, World-honored One,
Tathagata has the mind's eye."

"Subhuti, think about this:
Does Tathagata have the eyes of a Deva?"[26]

"Yes, World-honored One,
Tathagata has the eyes of all Devas."

"Subhuti, think about this:
Does Tathagata have the eyes of wisdom?"

26
Eyes of a Deva: This is
the ability to perceive
everything that Devas,
a type of heavenly
being, can perceive.

그렇습니다, 세존이시여

여래는 삼천대천세계 만물만생을

보는 사이 없이 다 보십니다.

수보리야, 어떻게 생각하느냐

여래에 법안法眼이 있겠느냐?

그렇습니다, 세존이시여.

여래는 우주 만물만생을 두루 비춰 아십니다.

수보리야, 어떻게 생각하느냐

여래에 불안佛眼이 있겠느냐?

그렇습니다, 세존이시여

일체 우주 만물만생의 움직임이 없이 움직임을

찰나에 다 아시고 보십니다.

"Yes, World-honored One,

Tathagata thoroughly sees all things

throughout all realms and universes,

with no moment of coming or going,

subject or object."

"Subhuti, think about this:

Does Tathagata have the eyes of Dharma?"

"Yes, World-honored One,

Tathagata can perceive and understand the functioning

of any being, any place, and any time

throughout the entire universe."

"Subhuti, think about this:

Does Tathagata have the eyes of a buddha?"

"Yes, World-honored One,

Tathagata instantly perceives everything throughout the universe,

as it moves and functions without any aspect of time or space."

수보리야, 어떻게 생각하느냐

갠지스강의 모래알같이

일체제불의 한마음의 부처가 그렇게 설했느냐?

그러합니다, 세존이시여.

여래는 저 모래알같이 응신으로 화하여

두루 아니 건지고 아니 설하심이 없으십니다.

수보리야, 어떻게 생각하느냐

한 갠지스강에 있는 모래 수와 같이

그만큼의 갠지스강이 있고

그 모든 갠지스강에 있는 모래 수만큼

많은 생명의 밝음이 있으며

"Subhuti, think about this:

Has Buddha,

which is the one mind of all buddhas,

taught in ways more varied than the sands of the Ganges?"

"Yes, World-honored One.

There are none Tathagata hasn't saved,

none Tathagata hasn't taught,

and no corner overlooked by Tathagata,

as it manifests and responds in ways more varied

than there are sands in the Ganges."

"Subhuti,

imagine if each grain of sand in the Ganges River

was itself another Ganges River.

Now, what if I were to tell you that the bright sparks of life

are as many as all the grains of sand in all of those rivers,

이 모든 공空안에

그 모래 수만큼의 불세계가 있다면

얼마나 많다고 하겠느냐?

매우 많습니다, 세존이시여.

부처님께서 수보리에게 이르시되

저 국토 가운데 있는

중생의 천차만별 종류의 마음을

여래는 다 알고 응해 주시느니

and that in the midst of the flowing, formless whole,

all of those bright sparks

are ceaselessly connecting and interacting,

and that the number of those interactions, those Buddha realms,[27]

is likewise more than all of the sands of those Ganges Rivers?

How many do you think that would be?”

“Such a number would indeed be great, World-honored One.”

“Subhuti, know this:

Throughout all of these realms,

Tathagata perceives the minds of all beings,

their many and varied functioning,

the level of their existence,

and responds accordingly.

27
Buddha realms:
Buddha realm, Buddha
land, and Buddha's
Pure Land all appear to
mean the same thing.

무슨 까닭인가?

여래가 천차만별의 마음들에게 설한 모든 마음이

마음이 아니고

그 이름이 마음인 것이니라.

까닭은 무엇인가, 수보리야.

과거심도 현재심

미래심도 현재심

현재심도 현재심으로 가득 차 공한 까닭이니라.

All of the responses to every kind of being and situation

are manifestations of this formless whole,

working as one.

Thus, even 'mind' and 'response' are just convenient labels,

for Tathagata is, in fact,

the all encompassing, flowing whole,

where the minds of all beings from the past are here now,

where the minds of all beings of the future are here now,

and where the minds of all beings of the present are here now."

19 / 법계를 두루 찰나찰나 화함이니라

Chapter 19

Becoming one with the entire Dharma realm and ceaselessly manifesting far and wide

수보리야, 어떻게 생각하느냐.

만약 어떤 사람이 삼천대천세계를

둘 아닌 한마음의 칠보 보배로 가득 채워

보이는 사람, 안 보이는 중생, 일체 만민에게

넣어도 두드러지지 않고

꺼내도 줄지 않는 보시를 한다면

이 사람은 이 인연으로 복을 받음이 많겠느냐?

"Subhuti,

imagine if someone were to fill the entire,

vast universe,

with the seven treasures

of this nondual one mind,[28]

and then offered these to everyone,

including both people who can perceive these treasures,

as well as those unenlightened beings who are unaware of them.

If someone were to give like this,

from this nondual one mind,

which never overflows no matter how much is put into it,

and which never decreases no matter how much is given,

then as a result of this karmic affinity,

do you think they would receive many blessings?"

[28] **Seven treasures of nondual one mind**: These are unspecified, but likely refer to the ability of our fundamental mind to positively affect people and the world around us.

그렇습니다, 세존이시여.

이 사람은 이 인연에 의해

일체 만유萬有의 둘이 아닌 공덕이 되겠습니다.

수보리야,

만약 공덕이 정말 있을진댄

여래가 공덕을 얻었다고 설하지 않았을 것이다.

공덕이 공한 까닭에 없으니

여래는 공덕이 크다고 말하느니라.

"Indeed, World-honored One,

through such karmic affinity,

a person would create the virtue and merit

that will allow them to become one,

one with everything in the universe."

"Subhuti,

Tathagata said that they obtain vast virtue and merit

not because there is some separate thing

to be called 'virtue and merit,'

but because becoming one with everything

and functioning together as one

is itself virtue and merit."

20 / 색色과 상相을 여읨이니

Chapter 20

Breaking away from appearances and perceptions

수보리야, 어떻게 생각하느냐

부처란 색신을 갖춘 것으로 볼 수 있겠느냐?

아니옵니다, 세존이시여.

여래를 구족^{具足}한 색신이라고 보지 못합니다.

왜냐하면 여래가 설하는 구족색신이란

곧 구족한 색신이 아니기에

구족색신이라 이름하는 것입니다.

수보리야, 어떻게 생각하느냐

여래를 일체 상이 구족한 것으로 볼 수 있겠느냐?

"What do you think, Subhuti?
Can you look at a buddha
and see the physical manifestation of Tathagata?"

"No, World-honored One,
Tathagata cannot be perceived by means of
physical form or appearance.
What people think of as the appearance of Tathagata,
is not the 'complete appearance' that Tathagata speaks of.
It is called 'the complete appearance of Tathagata'
because Tathagata manifests in every kind of way,
according to the need."

"Subhuti,
do you think that there are concepts or awareness that would
allow someone to recognize Tathagata?"

아니옵니다, 세존이시여.

여래를 보려면 구족한 상으로는 볼 수 없습니다.

왜냐하면 여래가 설하는 것은

일체 상으로 구족한 것이 곧 구족이 아니라

그 이름이 제상구족諸相具足인 때문입니다.

"No, World-honored One,

if someone wants to know Tathagata,

they cannot do so through their ideas or

perceptions of its apparent characteristics.

For, the manifested aspects of Tathagata

are not the essence of Tathagata.

Those are just called 'the complete manifestation of Tathagata'

because Tathagata responds fully and perfectly[29] to all beings."

29
Perfectly: The response
is perfect in the sense that
it is what is best suited
to the level of being's
functioning, their karma,
and their spiritual ability.

21 / 마음과 마음으로 통하는 설법이니라

Chapter 21

Teachings that come from mind, connecting with mind

수보리야,

너는 여래가 생각을 하되

내가 마땅히 설한 바 법이 있다고 말하지 말라.

왜냐하면 만약에 어떤 사람이 말하되

여래가 설한 바 없이 설한 까닭에

법이 있다고 한다면

곧 부처님을 비방함이니

지혜롭게 설한 바 없이 설한 바를

내가 알지 못하는 까닭이니라.

수보리야,

설법이란 것은

함이 없이 설한 법이니

설한 바 없음을 이름하여 법이라 하느니라.

"Subhuti,
do not think that Tathagata believes that,

'What has been taught by me is, of course, the truth.'

Likewise, if someone says,

'What Tathagata teaches is done while one with everything,

and thus, is the truth,'

then they slander the Buddha,

and have not understood

that which has been wisely taught

from the combined functioning of everything as one.

"Subhuti,

such teachings are a flowing exchange,

with nothing separate that could be labeled 'teachings.'

Thus, it is called the truth."

그때 혜명慧命 수보리가 부처님께 사뢰었다.

세존이시여,

어떤 중생이 미래세 오늘에

이 법을 설함을 듣고서 믿는 마음을 내겠습니까?

부처님께서 말씀하시되

수보리야,

저들은 오늘의 중생과 다름없어

중생이 아니며

중생이 아님도 아니니라.

무슨 까닭인가, 수보리야.

중생, 중생이란 여래가 설하되,

중생이라 함은 중생이 아니라

그 이름이 중생이니라.

Subhuti, who valued wisdom above all else, asked the Buddha,

"World-honored One,

in future ages,

in this ever-present 'now,'

will there be any unenlightened beings,

who, upon hearing this teaching,

will have faith in it?"

The Buddha replied,

"Subhuti,

those unenlightened beings will be no different

from the beings of today:

not unenlightened beings,

but also not something other than unenlightened beings.

"Why is this, Subhuti?

'Unenlightened beings' is just a label,

not a description of their fundamental essence."

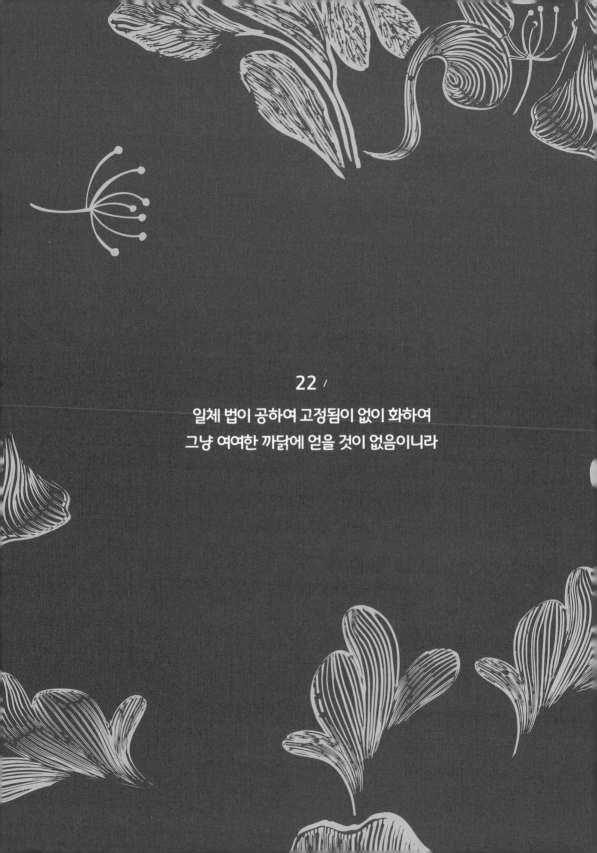

22 /

일체 법이 공하여 고정됨이 없이 화하여
그냥 여여한 까닭에 얻을 것이 없음이니라

Chapter 22

All things are connected through the foundation, and function
as one whole, ceaselessly transforming, with no fixed form,
and are just flowing without hindrance.
Thus, there is nothing to gain.

22. 일체 법이 공하여 고정됨이 없이 화하여
그냥 여여한 까닭에 얻을 것이 없음이니라

수보리가 부처님께 사뢰되

세존이시여,

부처님께서 위없는 진실한 마음을 얻은 마음은

얻은 바 없음이 되는지요?

부처님께서 말씀하시되

일체가 둘이 아니게 화하여

고정됨이 없이 나투는 까닭에

얻은 바 없다 하였느니

그러하고 그러하다, 수보리야.

내가 위없는 진실한 한마음을 깨우쳤다 함도,

내지는 작은 법이라도

공한 까닭에 얻음이 없음이라 하느니

위없이 깨우침도 공하므로

공까지도 이름이니라.

Subhuti asked the Buddha,

"World-honored One,

am I correct in understanding that

when you attained the utmost, profound awareness,

there was nothing you gained?"

The Buddha replied,

"Indeed, indeed, Subhuti.

All things are ceaselessly transforming

utterly free of any discrimination,

manifesting with no fixed aspect,

so there was nothing I could claim to have gained.

In awakening to this unsurpassed, profound one mind,

as well as to all lesser states and awarenesses,

there was only the flowing whole,

ceaselessly transforming and manifesting, with no fixed aspect.

Thus, there was nothing to gain.

Even the 'emptiness' of this supreme awakening,

is just a label."

23 /

내면과 물질세계가 둘이 아닌 마음으로 선善을 행함이니

Chapter 23

*Realizing that all inner and outer things work together nondually,
go forward putting this into practice*

다시 말하되 수보리야,

이 법은 평등하여 높고 낮음이 없으므로

이를,

위없이 공 아닌 공하였음을 깨우침이라 이름하나니

"**S**ubhuti,
let me repeat:

This nondual functioning of all things

applies to absolutely everything, equally.

It is the same throughout all realms,

and all levels of understanding and awakening.

Thoroughly knowing this nondual oneness,

this all-pervading truth,

is to have awakened to the supreme emptiness that is the whole,

working as one, ceaselessly transforming and manifesting.

"Thus, if you truly put this wonderful practice

of entrusting into action,

taking everything and returning it inwardly,

knowing that everything functions as one whole

through your foundation,

나도 없고 사람도 없고 중생도 없고 수자도 없이

나로 인하여 공하였음을

내면에 일체 놓고

선법善法을 닦아 행하면

곧 위없는 평등공법을 깨우쳐 얻으리라.

수보리야,

말한 바 선법이란 여래가 설하되

곧 선법이 아닌 선법이니라.

such that there is no 'me,'

no 'humans,' [30]

no 'unenlightened beings,'

nor 'beings on the path of awakening,'

then most assuredly,

your eyes will open to

the principle of nonduality,

this truth of great oneness,

which encompasses absolutely everything,

and functions everywhere.

"Subhuti,

the nondual returning and entrusting of all things,

as taught by Tathagata,

is not some separate thing,

it is the nondual functioning of oneness."

[30] **Humans:** The nuance appears to be the idea of "humans, as the beings most able to awaken among those beings with physical bodies."

24 /
복덕도 지혜도 둘이 아니었음이니라

Chapter 24

*Both the wisdom and the good fortune that result from
nondual actions and thought turn out to be ultimately
the same thing*

수보리야,

만약 어떤 사람이

삼천대천세계 가운데 있는

일체 공세계의 한마음의 공덕을 가지고

칠보로 보시한다면

일체가 둘이 아닌 까닭에

보시한 사이가 없음이니라.

"Subhuti,
if someone, using the virtue and merit of one mind,

which exists throughout all realms of this flowing whole,

should give the energy of the seven treasures of mind

to help others,

then, because all things are not two,

there is, in fact, no separation between giver and receiver,

nor is there anything that is given.

만약 어떤 사람이

반야바라밀의 둘이 아닌 경의 말씀으로써

사구게가 따로 없는 밝은 마음으로 받아

내면에 지니고 읽고 외워서

남을 위해 설한다면

앞도 뒤도 없는 공덕의 칠보 보시란

백분의 일도 없고

백천만억분의 일도 없음이니

숫자로 비유할 수 없어

능히 미치지 못하였으므로

공함이라 했느니라.

"If someone

accepts these nondual teachings of

this all-embracing oneness,

this supreme wisdom,

and sees beyond the words and letters,

accepting it with a clear, shining mind,

reflecting inwardly upon these teachings,

engraving them within their very bones,

and teaches them for the benefit of others,

then, because these treasures of mind that they are giving

arise from the beginningless and endless virtue and merit

of everything functioning as one,

it can't be said that any help has been given,

not even the tiniest bit.

The effects of this giving

are beyond anything that can be measured,

thus it's simply called 'emptiness.'"

25 /

교화하되 교화함이 없이 함이니

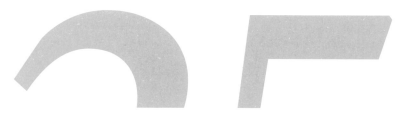

Chapter 25

Teaching and guiding through the foundation, with no giver or receiver

수보리야, 어떻게 생각하느냐.

들어라.

여래께서 생각했다 말하지 말라.

나는 중생을 제도하되

생각 없이 함이 없이 함이니라.

수보리야,

생각 없이 생각함이니

생각 내었다 하지 말라.

왜냐하면

공심·공용·공체·공식하며

찰나찰나 화하여 끝 간 데 없음이니

여래가 제도할 중생이 없음이라 함이니라.

260

"**S**ubhuti,
pay attention:

Do not say that Tathagata gives rise to intentions of

leading beings out of ignorance.

When Tathagata guides beings,

it does so without any thoughts of guiding them,

without any 'them' or 'me.'

"Subhuti,

Tathagata's thoughts arise free of discriminations,

working as one with everything,

so don't think that Tathagata is deliberately giving rise

to intentions of helping.

For, all beings have this foundation,

and through it, all are connected as one,

working together as one,

and giving and receiving whatever is needed

while ceaselessly transforming every instant.

For this same reason,

there are no separate beings for Tathagata to aid.

만약 여래가 제도할 중생이 있어

"내가 제도했다" 한다면

여래가 아니니라.

여래는 곧 한마음을 지닌 사람,

즉 중생이자 수자가 있음이니라.

수보리야,

여래가 설하되 내가 있음이란

곧 내가 있음이 아니라 함이니라.

범부들은 내가 있다고 생각하지만

수보리야,

범부라는 것이 여래가 설하되

곧 부처 범부가 따로 없음이라,

부처 범부란 이름이니라.

"If there is the thought,

'There were beings who needed guidance,

thus I helped them,'

then this is not Tathagata.

For, Tathagata always exists as one mind,

and this flowing one mind already encompasses

all of those beings who are struggling in darkness,

as well as those on the path of awakening.

"Thus, Subhuti,

although Tathagata has spoken of Tathagata,

know that Tathagata is not something that exists separately,

for Tathagata is ever-flowing oneness,

ceaselessly transforming, manifesting, and responding.

Ordinary people think that there is a Tathagata

that exists apart from themselves,

but know, Subhuti,

there is no separate 'buddha' or 'ordinary person.'

Both 'buddha' and 'ordinary person' are just labels."

26 / 법신은 상相이 아님이니라

Chapter 26

The manifestations of Tathagata do not have fixed forms

수보리야, 어떻게 생각하느냐

삼십이상으로써

여래를 볼 수 있다고 하겠느냐?

수보리가 말씀드리되

아니옵니다, 아니옵니다.

삼십이상으로써 여래를 볼 수 없습니다.

"Subhuti,
what do you think?

Can Tathagata be recognized

by means of things like the thirty-two aspects?"

Subhuti answered,

"No, no.

Tathagata cannot be perceived by means of manifestations

such as the thirty-two aspects."

부처님께서 말씀하시되

수보리야,

만약 삼십이상으로써 여래를 본다면

전륜성왕도 여래라고 하리라.

수보리가 부처님께 사뢰었다.

세존이시여,

제가 부처님의 설하신 바 뜻을 이해하기로는

응당 삼십이상으로써 여래를 알 수 없습니다.

The Buddha said,

"Subhuti,

if the thirty-two aspects indicated someone was Tathagata,

then you could claim that even the leader of a country was

Tathagata."[31]

Subhuti spoke to the Buddha,

"World-honored One,

hearing this, I am certain that

it is not through manifestations or

features such as the thirty-two aspects

that Tathagata can be known."

31
Leader as Tathagata: While the thirty-two aspects are often given literal, physical descriptions, such as long fingers, long ears, flat feet, and so on, they are considered the manifestations of spiritual power, and so are symbolic of that ability.

A sweet, appealing body odor could be compared to charisma. Having long fingers can be thought of as the power to reach everywhere. Having long ears could be thought of as the ability to hear everything, and so on. For this reason, Seon Master Daehaeng has compared these to the far-reaching powers of secular leaders.

그때 세존께서 게송으로 설하셨다.

"만약 색신으로 나를 보거나

음성으로 나를 구하면

그런 사람은 삿된 도를 행함이라

능히 여래를 보지 못하리라."

With this, the Buddha spoke the following verse:

> *If someone tries to recognize me*
>
> *by the form of my body,*
>
> *if they are searching for me*
>
> *by the sound of my voice,*
>
> *then they are practicing false ways,*
>
> *and will be incapable of recognizing Tathagata.*

27 / 끊는 것도 없고 멸함도 없음이니

Chapter 27

There is no "ceasing" or "extinguishing"

수보리야,

네가 이런 생각을

함이 없이 하되 여래는 구족한 상이 없이 하는 까닭에

위없고 진실한 한마음의 깨달음을

얻었다 생각하는가?

수보리야,

세상이 공하여 함이 없이 여여한데,

얻었다 생각하지 말라.

여래는 구족하다는 상을 내지 않고

함이 없이 하는 까닭에

위없이 공한 진리의 한마음을

깨달아 얻었다고 말하리라.

"Subhuti,
would you think that because Tathagata does all things working as one whole, free of any thought of 'I am doing…,' and fully responding and manifesting according to the need, that this indicates that Tathagata has gained the supreme, profound enlightenment of one mind?

"Subhuti,
all this world inherently works and flows as one whole,
functioning without divisions,
so do not think that there is something that's gained.
However, there are people who see that Tathagata
responds and manifests fully,
without any trace of 'I'm doing,'
becoming one with whatever arises,
and, so, say that this indicates that Tathagata
has obtained the supreme enlightenment of one mind.

수보리야,

네가 만약 그런 생각을 하되

위없는 진실한 한마음을 깨달은 자는

일체 법을 단멸하게 설한다고

생각하지 말라.

왜냐하면 위없는 진실한 한마음을 깨달은 자는

법에 있어서 단멸상을 말하지 않느니라.

"Further, Subhuti,

although you, too, may still think

there is something that's gained,

do not think that someone who has awakened

to this utterly genuine, supreme oneness

teaches about gaining or cutting off.

For, those who have awakened

to this supremely profound one mind,

would never speak of the true functioning of all things,

in terms of gaining, ceasing, or extinguishing."[32]

32
Ceasing or extinguishing:
This is the idea that
getting rid of or cutting off
delusions is a way of gaining
enlightenment.

28 / 받지도 않고 탐하지도 않음이니

Chapter 28   *Neither receiving nor coveting*

수보리야,

만약 보살이

갠지스강 모래 수 같은 세계에 가득 찬

한마음의 칠보로써

우주 만물만생

천차만별의 중생들에게 보시하더라도

함이 없는 함이라야

진정한 보시이니라.

만약 어떤 사람이 있어

일체 법이 무아無我임을 알아

인忍을 얻어 이루면

"Subhuti,
even if a bodhisattva offers

all the seven treasures of one mind,

from worlds as many

as the sands of the Ganges,

for the benefit of every kind of being across

the entire universe,

this must be done while one with everything,

free of thoughts of self and other.

Then, it can become a true offering.

"If someone understands

that everything in the universe functions

together as one,

without any separately existing self,[33]

and then, with perseverance and sincerity,

they apply themselves

and attain enlightenment,

33
Without any separately
existing self: Literally,
"All things have no self"
(諸法無我). There are
a number of nuances
in this expression. One
is that, although we
each have bodies and
consciousness, these, too,
are collections and the
results of the interplay of
the interdependent whole
that we are part of.
 In addition, we are
constantly being shaped
by our circumstances,
relationships, and affinities
with the world around
us. All of these, too, are
constantly changing as
well. There is no "self"
that exists apart or
unchanged by all of this.
 This is why in
Buddhism, the term
"ignorance" refers to
a lack of awareness
of this. It is thinking
that in the midst of this
interconnected flowing,
there is a separate "me"
that exists apart from
everything else.

이 앞뒤 없는 보살은

어디다 비교할 수 없는

공덕이라는 이름 없는 공덕을 얻으리라.

왜냐하면 수보리야,

일체 보살은

만물만생 천차만별이 다 공한 까닭에

공덕을 얻었다고 하지 않는 까닭이니라.

then such a bodhisattva,

such an utterly unconfined bodhisattva,

such an all-encompassing bodhisattva,

will have attained virtue and merit

that is utterly beyond what people think of

as virtue and merit.

"Subhuti,

but even in this,

all things and lives,

all states and realms of existence,

exist as this interconnected, flowing whole,

functioning together without any fixed form or state,

so it cannot even be said that bodhisattvas obtain

virtue and merit."

수보리가 부처님께 사뢰었다.

세존이시여,

어찌하여 보살은 공덕을 받지 않습니까?

수보리야,

보살은

시공을 초월하여 일체가 둘이 아닌 까닭에

공덕에 탐착함이 없으니

그런고로 공덕을 받지 않는다고 설하는 것이니라.

Subhuti asked the Buddha,

"World-honored One,

how could it be that bodhisattvas

do not receive virtue and merit?"

"Subhuti,

everything functions as one,

with no separately existing place or time.

Bodhisattvas exist fully within this functioning of the whole,

and so no craving for things such as virtue and merit arises.

Because they are not captivated by such craving,

they don't receive the results of it."

29 / 위없는 고요함이니

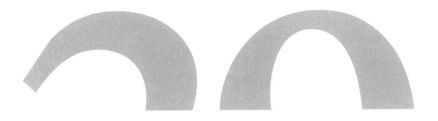

Chapter 29   *Ultimate serenity*

수보리야,

만약 어떤 사람이 말하기를

여래는 오고 감이 없이 오고 가며,

앉고 눕는 사이 없이

앉고 누움이 여여하다고 한다면

이 사람은 내가 설한 바 뜻을 알지 못함이니

일체가 여래 아닌 바가 없어서

여래는 어디로부터 온 바가 없고

또 갈 바도 없는 까닭에

이름을 여래라 하느니라.

"Subhuti, should someone say that

Tathagata goes forth into the world

manifesting as one with everything,

doing everything in life naturally, as one,

then, Subhuti,

such a person has not understood what I have taught.

For the entire whole, working as one, is itself Tathagata.

Tathagata never comes from somewhere else,

nor goes to someplace else,

thus, the name 'Tathagata' is given." [34]

34
Tathagata: The traditional translation from Sanskrit of "Tathagata" is "Thus come," but given the context here, just "Thusness" might be a more fitting interpretation.

30 / 끝없는 진리와 현상은 하나임이니

Chapter 30

All phenomena are the ceaseless workings of everything as one whole

수보리야,

만약 어떤 지혜 있는 남녀가

삼천대천세계를 부숴서 티끌로 만든다면

어떻게 생각하느냐?

무無의 중생 유有의 중생,

일체 천차만별이 헤아릴 수 없이 티끌 같은데

어찌 많다고 하지 않겠느냐.

"Subhuti,
imagine if all realms and universes

were broken down into dust particles.

All the living patterns of energy[35]

throughout the visible realms as well as the unseen realms,

are as varied and uncountable

as all of those tiny pieces.

That seems like a lot, doesn't it?"

35
Living patterns of energy:
The original word used here,
衆生, is often translated as
"sentient being," or sometimes
"unawakened being," but the
context indicates something
more fundamental that
transcends definitions of
existence based on matter or
biochemical processes.

수보리가 말씀드리되

매우 많습니다, 세존이시여.

왜냐하면 이 많은 티끌들이

실제로 다 있는 것이라면

부처님께서는

곧 많은 티끌이라고 설하지 않았을 것입니다.

그 까닭이 무엇인가 하면

부처님께서 설하신 많은 티끌은 곧 티끌이 아니라

그 이름이 티끌입니다.

세존이시여,

여래께서 설하신 바

삼천대천세계는 곧 세계가 아니고

그 이름이 세계입니다.

294

Subhuti spoke,

"Indeed, World-honored One,

that is a great amount.

However, what the Buddha speaks of

is the true nature of their existence,

not the appearance that they seem to have in this world.

All of the words used to describe those different aspects

are just convenient labels.

"World-honored One,

reflecting upon what Tathagata has taught,

I realize that what people think of as universes

is a misunderstanding,

for 'realms' and 'universes' are merely the labels used.

왜냐하면 세계가 실로 있는 것이라면

곧 둥근 모양이니

여래가 설하신 것은

공하여 하나로 시공을 초월해

찰나에 화하여 나툴 뿐

이름이 붙지 않습니다.

곧 둥근 원리가

하나로 들고 하나로 나는 진리도

이름이 원의 진리인 때문입니다.

수보리야,

하나로 합한 진리란

말로는 설할 수 없느니라.

다만 범부들이 이론과 이름, 말에 탐착할 뿐이니라.

That which people try to apply such labels to,

functions as one harmonious whole.

What Tathagata has spoken of is emptiness,

where everything is working together as one whole,

where there is only ceaseless transformation and manifestation,

beyond any limited perceptions of time or place,

and to which no labels can be applied.

In other words,

this principle of flowing oneness

is the truth that everything

arises from oneness

and returns to oneness.

Even 'the truth of oneness'

is merely words used for the sake of a name."

"Truly, Subhuti,

words cannot describe this truth,

which is the combined functioning of everything as one.

Nonetheless, ordinary people still cling to

theories, labels, and descriptions."

31 / 지견을 내지 않음이니

Chapter 31

Not giving rise to thoughts of "knowing"

수보리야,

어떤 사람이 말하기를

부처님이 아견·인견·중생견·수자견을 설하였다 하면

수보리야, 어떻게 생각하느냐

이 사람은

내가 설한 바 뜻을 알았다 하겠느냐?

아니옵니다, 세존이시여.

이 사람은

여래께서 설하신 바 뜻을 알지 못합니다.

왜냐하면 세존이시여,

세존이 설한 아견·인견·중생견·수자견은

곧 아견·인견·중생견·수자견이 아니라

그 이름이 아견·인견·중생견·수자견입니다.

"Subhuti,
should someone say that,

'The Buddha is teaching

about self,

about humanity and its potential,

about unenlightened beings,

and about the limitations and potential of this life and this body,'

then, Subhuti,

has such a person understood what I've been saying?"

"No, World-honored One,

such a person

has not understood Tathagata.

Even though the Buddha spoke of self,

of unenlightened beings, of the nature of humanity,

and of the potential and nature of our existence,

those words were just labels."

수보리야,

위없는 진실한 한마음을 깨우친 사람은

일체 법에 있어 응당 둘이 아니게 화하여

고정됨이 없이 나툴 뿐의 도리를 알며

이와 같이 보며 이와 같이 믿어서

법이라는 상을 내지 말라.

수보리야,

말한 바 법상이라는 것은

여래가 설하되

곧 모든 법상이 아니고

그 이름이 법상인 것이니라.

"Subhuti,

one who has awakened

to this supreme, profound, utterly authentic one mind,

perceives that everything is an interconnected whole,

ceaselessly transforming,

manifesting free of any fixed forms.

So, see everything in this way,

have faith that it all is working in this way,

and don't give rise to fixed concepts

about truth

or how things work.

"Subhuti,

although people think of these ideas

as the teachings of Tathagata,

know that all of those

are merely labels."

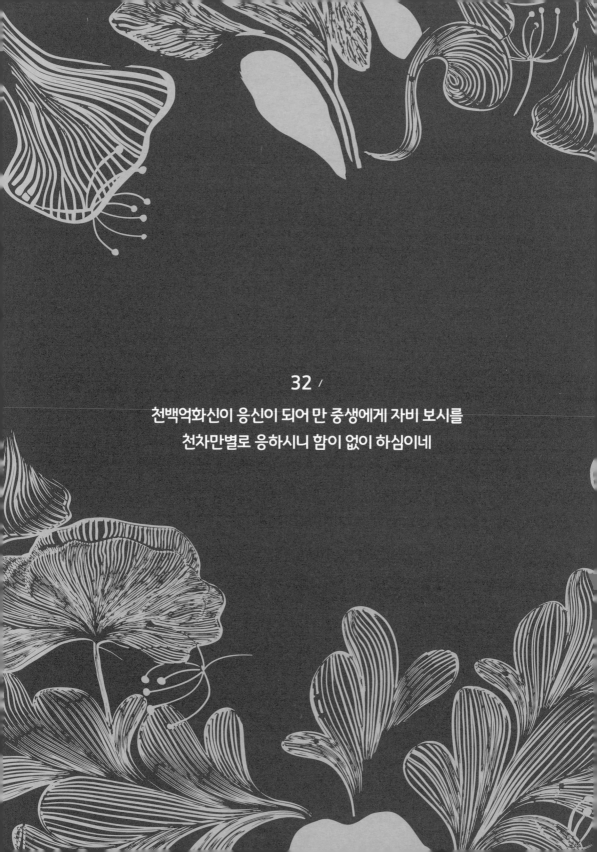

32 /

천백억화신이 응신이 되어 만 중생에게 자비 보시를
천차만별로 응하시니 함이 없이 하심이네

Chapter 32

Unconditionally helping every kind of being by responding from the whole in billions of different ways

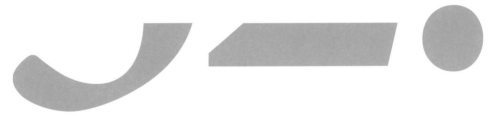

수보리야,

만약 어떤 사람이 있어

한량없는 아승지 아닌 아승지 세계에 가득 찬

칠보 아닌 칠보로써

조건 없이 보시를 한다면,

함이 없는 보시라야 진정한 보시니라.

만약 어떤 지혜 있는 남녀가

보살의 마음을 내어 자비로

선과 경을 둘이 아니게 내면에 지니되

사구게 아닌 사구게 등을

내면에 지니고 독송하게 한다면

공덕이 크고 크니라.

"Subhuti,
if someone uses the vast treasures

of the uncountable, boundless realms of mind,

using them unconditionally,

for the sake of others,

then this is giving as one,

this is true giving.

"Keep giving rise

to the heart of a bodhisattva,

to unconditional compassion,

and inwardly, nondually,

make these teachings and your practice as one.

Help those who wish to learn these teachings

that are not teachings[36]

to learn them from this inner, nondual place.

If you do so, the virtue and merit of this will be truly great.

36
Learning teachings
that are not teachings:
Literally, "if they wish
to recite verses that
are not verses." In past
ages, recitation was how
something new was
learned, so the nuance
is closer to "learn
something deeply,"
rather than merely
chanting.

남을 위해 설한다면

과거 현재 미래, 삼세 가운데

칠보 보시보다 더 큰 공덕을 얻으리라.

어떻게 남을 위해 설하는가.

나를 세우지 말고

여여하게 한마음으로 진실하게 하라.

"If, for the sake of others,

you teach and guide them,

then the virtue and merit of that will be greater than

if you had spent the past, present, and future

giving all of the seven treasures.

"How should you teach so that others benefit?

Avoid falling into 'me' or 'I am doing,'

into subtle pride, arrogance, or resentment,

and instead work to become one with them,

seeing them as yourself,

teaching them accordingly,

selflessly,

sincerely,

unconditionally.

일체 물질세계는 환상 같고,

물거품 같고,

이슬 같고,

번개 같으니

응당 내가 있어서 상대가 있음이라.

용도에 따라 닥치는 대로

내면에 놓고 관할지어다.

"The entire material world is like a dream,

an illusion,

like bubbles on the waves,

like dew,

like a flash of lightning,

and all of it arises and responds

in accord with you yourself.

So in whatever situation you find yourself,

with whatever confronts you,

with whatever is needed,

entrust all of this inwardly,

and continue to observe

while trusting your nondual foundation."

부처님께서 안과 밖이 없는 경설을

무심의 도리로 마치시니

장로 수보리와 여러 비구 비구니

우바새 우바이 여러 대중과

일체 세간 천상 인간 아수라 등이

부처님께서 설하신 바를 듣고

모두 크게 환희하며

믿고 받들어 행하도다.

When the Buddha,

connecting and communicating as one with all beings,

finished teaching this truth of emptiness,

the functioning of everything as one,

where everything functions as one whole,

with no beginning or end,

no inside or outside,

nor fixed form of any kind,

the preeminent bhikkhu, Subhuti,

and the many other bhikkhus and bhikkhunis,

laymen and laywomen,

of the entire assembly,

together with all beings

throughout the heavenly realms,

the human realms,

and the lower realms,

having heard what the Buddha taught,

were all filled with bliss.

Having faith in what the Buddha said,

taking to heart what the Buddha said,

they all proceeded to put those teachings

into action.

결^結

꽃이 피고 열매 맺어
대행큰스님

갖은 꽃이 갖은 꽃이

피고 지고

피고 지고

피고 져서,

지고 피고

열매가 맺으니

제 나무에서

좁지 않고 넓지 않게 익어서

다들 응신으로서 응신들이,

Blossoming and Ripening

Seon Master Daehaeng

Flowers, flowers,

flowers of every kind

bloom and fade,

bloom and fade,

bloom and fade,

fade and bloom,

at last bearing fruit.

There, on each tree,

is where this fruit will fully ripen,

ripening perfectly for that tree,

neither too small nor too big,

neither too narrow nor too diffuse.

As the fruit ripens thus,

it will manifest as the essence of its true root,

responding to beings of every kind,

다 갖은 중생들이

제 나무에서 무르익은 걸

먹고 주고 먹고

응신의 수기를 받아서 잘해 나가면

이 세상이 편안하고

우주가, 일체가 다 편안하다.

각색의 꽃이 피고 지는 대로,

지는 대로 열매 맺으면

그 열매는

제 나무에서 익어야 제 맛이 나네.

helping them to ripen the fruit of their own tree,

such that their own fruit will feed them

as well as everyone around them,

ceaselessly feeding, giving, receiving.

Having thus received assurance

of this role and potential,

if you, too, go forward helping others like this,

working at becoming one with everything,

then this world will become at peace,

the universe will become at peace,

everyone will become at peace.

As every kind of flower

blooms and fades,

fades and bears fruit,

that fruit must ripen on its own tree,

in order for its true flavor to appear.

닫는 글

대행큰스님의 뜻으로 푼 『금강경』은 여러분을 변화시킵니다. 처음엔 눈치채지 못하겠지만, 정말 그렇습니다. 금강경은 진리를 완전히 깨달은 자와 그의 수제자 사이에서 오고 가는 대화로 되어 있는데, 그 대화가 여러분이 생각할 수 있는 사고의 범위를 훌쩍 벗어나 있을 때조차도 여러분은 거기에 스며들게 됩니다.

금강경을 영어로 옮기기 위해 우리가 마주 앉았을 때, 처음엔 대략 1년, 길게는 2년 정도 걸릴 거라 생각했습니다. 매번 번역작업이 끝날 때마다 우리는 꽤 괜찮게 했다고 느꼈지만, 어느덧 세월은 9년이 지났고, 수정본이 24권이나 쌓이게 되었습니다! 한글 원문에 내포되어 있는 의미를 곰곰이 생각해보고 그 뜻을 살리는 가장 좋은 영어 표현을 고민하는 과정에서 우린 실로 많은 것을 배웠습니다. 그러면서 우리는 변해갔습니다. 그 변화는 미세해서 포착하기 힘들었지만, 언제부턴가 세상에 대한 이해와 세상을 바라보는 우리의 시각이 달라져 갔습니다.

이번이 마지막 검토라고 생각하고 모일 때마다, 우리는 한글 원문이 품고 있는 더 깊은 의미와 미처 파악하지 못했던 뜻을 발견했고, 영어번역을 광범위하게 다시 써 내려가야 하는 상황이 연출되곤 하였습니다. 그럼에도 문장이

Afterword

Seon Master Daehaeng's edition of the *Diamond Sutra* changes you. You won't notice it at first, but it does. It's a conversation between two people who have already tasted this nondual whole, and even when the conversation is beyond your perspective, it still soaks in.

When we sat down to translate this into English, we thought it might take us a year, maybe two at the outside. That was nine years and twenty-four drafts ago! Every time we finished a draft, we felt like we'd done a great job, that we had learned much as we reflected on the Korean text and discussed its implications and how best to express those in English. And we were changed. It was subtle, but our outlook and understanding of the world shifted. So that when we sat down again for what we thought was the final review of our translation, we started finding more nuances and ideas that required extensive rewrites of the English. And in those discussions and inward reflections on the meaning, we were further changed. Again and again this happened, for twenty-four drafts.

품고 있는 의미를 성찰해보고 멤버들과 토론해가는 과정에서 우리는 더 많은 변화를 겪었고, 이런 과정이 지속적으로 반복되다 보니 24차례나 수정된 원고가 나오게 된 것이지요.

겉으로 드러나지는 않았지만, 우리는 각자 한글 원문이 무엇을 말하고 있는지를 내면에 묻고 그 답을 찾으려고 노력했던 것 같습니다. 의문나는 점들이 마음 속 깊이 가라앉도록 맡겨 두면서, 어떤 해답이 나오게 될지 조용히 기다렸습니다. 모두가 이렇게 할 때면, 번역작업이 꽤 잘 진행되었고, 깊은 영감을 자아내는 영어표현들이 떠오르곤 했습니다. 우리가 문장의 자구^{字句}해석에만 갇혀 있거나, 우리 인식범위의 사각지대에 놓여 있는 뉘앙스를 표현해 내기 어려워 갑갑함 속에 빠져 있을 때, 작업은 아주 어색하고 느리게 흘러갔습니다.

이 과정에서 우리가 배운 점을 한가지 언급하자면, 우리가 하고 있는 일이 무엇이든지 간에 모든 것을 다잡아서, 일체가 둘 아니게 돌아가는 내면의 근본마음에 "맡겨 놓는 것"이 정말 중요하다는 것입니다. 왜냐하면, 일체가 근본마음을 통해 서로 연결되어 상호작용하면서 끊임없이 바뀌어 돌아가는 한마음의 전체자리를 거쳐야, 인생과 세상을 바라보는 고정관념과 오래된 습^習으로부터 우리가 빠져나올 수 있기 때문이지요. 우리를 변화시키고, 우리가 상상해보지 못한 방식으로 우리를 자유롭게 해주는 것이 바로 둘 아니게 같이 돌아가는 이 한마음 도리의 묘미입니다.

It may not be apparent, but as we discussed what the Korean text might be saying, we also worked at asking these questions inwardly. We let them sink down within us, and then waited quietly to see what would come back out. When we were all doing this, the work went quite well and the English expressions seemed particularly inspired. When we got caught up in the words and frustrations of trying to explain the nuances that were edging around the corners of our awareness, the work was awkward and slow.

If we had to point out just one thing we learned from this process, it would be the importance of taking on whatever we are doing while trying to entrust that task to this nondual foundation within us. For it is only through this connection that is the ever-changing whole that we can step out of our habits and fixed ways of thinking about life and the world. It is this taste of the whole that changes us and frees us in ways we could never have imagined.

Imagine what might happen if someone practices like this while reading an expression of this nondual whole?

At its core, the *Diamond Sutra* is an expression of this whole, manifesting as nondual love. It's the love Subhuti felt for all

이런 가르침을 읽고 깊이 생각해 보면서, 그 가르침을 실천하는 노력을 꾸준히 해 나아가다 보면, 자신이 간절히 원하던 더 깊이 있고 진화된 나의 모습을 보게 되지 않을까요?

금강경은 나와 상대를 둘로 보지 않는 진정한 사랑, 만물만생이 둘 아닌 마음으로 돌아가는 한마음의 도리에 대해 알려줍니다. 그것이 수보리가 모든 중생들이 겪고 있는 고통을 목도하고 그들이 깨달을 수 있도록 돕고자 했던 사랑이며, 석가모니 부처님께서 그 에너지에 응답하셨던 자비입니다.

이 책에서 말하고 있는 많은 부분들이 이해하기 어렵고 다소 낯설 수도 있겠지만, 일단은 담담히 내 안에 넣어 놔 보세요. 차츰 여러분을 변화시키고 무엇과도 비교할 수 없이 거대한 전체자리의 리듬에 맞추어 여러분의 삶이 조화롭게 흘러갈 수 있도록 도와줄 것입니다.

한마음국제문화원 일동 합장

beings as he saw them suffering and wanted to help them awaken, and it's the love that Shakyamuni Buddha had as he responded to that energy.

Much of what the *Diamond Sutra* talks about may be new to you, but if you quietly let it sink within you, it will change you and leave you more in touch with the rhythm of this incomparable whole that you are part of.

With palms together,

The Hanmaum International Culture Institute

대행큰스님에 대하여

대행큰스님은 여러 면에서 매우 보기 드문 선사禪師셨습니다. 비구스님이 지배적인 전통속에서 여성으로서 선사가 되셨고, 비구니스님들과 함께 비구스님들을 제자로 두셨으며, 젊은 세대의 청장년층 남녀들을 대거 신도계층으로 참여케 하여 한국불교에 새로운 풍격風格을 일으켰던 큰 스승이셨습니다. 또한 전통 비구니 강원과 종단에 지속적인 지원을 폄으로써 비구니 승단을 발전시키는데 중추적인 역할을 하셨습니다.

1927년 서울에서 태어난 스님은 일찍이 9세경에 자성을 밝히셨고, 당신이 증득하신 바를 완성하기 위해 10여 년이 넘는 세월을 산중에서 보내셨습니다. 훗날, 누더기가 다 된 해진 옷을 걸치고 손에 주어지는 것만을 먹으며 지냈던 그 당시를 회상하며 스님은 의도적으로 고행을 하고자 했던 것이 아니라, 당신에게 주어진 환경이 그러했노라고, 또한 근본 자성자리에 일체를 맡기고 그 맡긴 일이 어떻게 작용하는지를 관觀하는 일에 완전히 몰두하고 있었기에 다른 것에는 신경쓸 틈이 없었노라고 말씀하셨습니다.

About Seon Master Daehaeng

Daehaeng Kun Sunim[37] (1927-2012) was a rare teacher in Korea: a female Seon(Zen) master, a nun whose students included monks as well as nuns, and a teacher who helped revitalize Korean Buddhism by dramatically increasing the participation of young people and men. She broke out of traditional models of spiritual practice to teach in such a way that allowed anyone to practice and awaken, making laypeople a particular focus of her efforts. At the same time, she was a major force for the advancement of bhikkhunis, heavily supporting traditional nuns' colleges as well as the modern Bhikkhuni Council of Korea.

Born in Seoul, Korea, she awakened when she was around eight years old and spent the years that followed learning to put her understanding into practice. For years, she wandered the mountains of Korea, wearing ragged clothes and eating only what was at hand.

37
Kun Sunim: Seon Master Daehaeng was known to her students as "Kun Sunim," which is the title given in Korea to outstanding nuns and monks.

1950년대 말경, 스님은 산중 수행을 마치시고 치악산 상원사 근처에 있는 토굴에 머무르시며 수없는 사람들의 고통을 해결해 주셨습니다. 또한 스님은 사람들이 본래부터 무궁무진한 에너지와 지혜를 갖고 있음에도 그 역량을 알지 못해 고통을 겪으며 살아가는 현실에 대해 매우 안타까워하셨습니다.

마침내 스님은 1972년 경기도 안양에 한마음선원을 세우셨고 누구나 본래부터 가지고 있는 근본 자성인 '참나'를 믿고 의지해 살라는 가르침을 본격적으로 펼치기 시작하셨습니다. 이후 40여 년 동안 불법의 진리와 생활 속에서의 마음수행법을 가르치는 데 매진하셨으며, 현재 150여 명이 넘는 제자 스님들이 안양 본원과 25개의 국내외 지원에서 수행에 전념하고 있습니다. 대행큰스님은 2012년 5월 22일 입적하셨으며, 세납 86세, 법랍 63세셨습니다.

Later, she explained that she hadn't been pursuing some type of asceticism; rather, she was just completely absorbed in entrusting everything to her fundamental Buddha essence, and observing how that affected her life.

Those years profoundly shaped Kun Sunim's later teaching style; she intimately knew the great potential, energy, and wisdom inherent within each of us, and recognized that most of the people she encountered suffered because they didn't realize this about themselves. Seeing clearly the great light in every individual, she taught people to rely upon this inherent foundation, and refused to teach anything that distracted from this most important truth.

Her deep compassion made her a legend in Korea long before she formally started teaching. She was known for having the spiritual power to help people in all circumstances with every kind of problem. She compared compassion to freeing a fish from a drying puddle, putting a homeless family into a home, or providing the school fees that would allow a student to finish high school. And when she did things like this, and much more, few knew that she was behind it.

Kun Sunim saw that for people to live freely and go forward in the world as a blessing to all around them, they needed to know about this bright essence that is within each of us. To help people discover this for themselves, she founded the first Hanmaum Seon Center in 1972. For the next forty years she gave wisdom to those who needed wisdom, food and money to those who were poor and hungry, and compassion to those who were hurting.

※책에 관한 문의나 주문을 하실 분은 아래의 연락처로 문의해 주십시오.

한마음국제문화원/한마음출판사

(13908) 경기도 안양시 만안구 경수대로 1282
전화: (82-31) 470-3175
팩스: (82-31) 470-3209
이메일: onemind@hanmaum.org
hanmaumbooks.org
www.hanmaum.org

If you would like more information about these books or
would like to order copies of them,
please call or write to:

Hanmaum International Culture Institute

1282 Gyeongsu-daero, Manan-gu, Anyang-si,
Gyeonggi-do, 13908, Republic of Korea

hanmaumbooks.org
hanmaum.org/en
e-mail: onemind@hanmaum.org
Tel: (82-31) 470-3175
Fax: (82-31) 470-3209

03220

9 788991 857902